T0208218

# Joy in the
# Journey

MATHEW PHILIP

WESTBOW
PRESS®
A DIVISION OF THOMAS NELSON
& ZONDERVAN

WestBow Press books may be ordered through booksellers or by contacting:

WestBow Press
A Division of Thomas Nelson & Zondervan
1663 Liberty Drive
Bloomington, IN 47403
www.westbowpress.com
1 (866) 928-1240

Because of the dynamic nature of the Internet, any web addresses or links contained in this book may have changed since publication and may no longer be valid. The views expressed in this work are solely those of the author and do not necessarily reflect the views of the publisher, and the publisher hereby disclaims any responsibility for them.

Any people depicted in stock imagery provided by Getty Images are models, and such images are being used for illustrative purposes only. Certain stock imagery © Getty Images.

All Scripture quotations are taken from The Holy Bible, New International Version®, NIV® Copyright © 1973, 1978, 1984, 2011 by Biblica, Inc.® Used by permission. All rights reserved worldwide.

This book is a work of non-fiction. Unless otherwise noted, the author and the publisher make no explicit guarantees as to the accuracy of the information contained in this book and in some cases, names of people and places have been altered to protect their privacy. Some stories or news pieces in the book are from my memories of reading other books or online postings or from listening to speakers.

ISBN: 978-1-9736-5950-1 (sc)
ISBN: 978-1-9736-5952-5 (hc)
ISBN: 978-1-9736-5951-8 (e)

Library of Congress Control Number: 2019904644

Print information available on the last page.

WestBow Press rev. date: 5/7/2019

# CONTENTS

# ACKNOWLEDGMENTS

It takes a family to write a book, and this book is a product of friends and family members who shared their experiences in the journeys of life. The idea about life as a journey was further instilled in me when a dear friend who was diagnosed with cancer told me that it was the start of another journey within the journey of life.

Life is made up of little journeys whether it is starting school, getting married, having children, or taking a new job. Then there are other journeys that are not as exciting but painful in many cases—diagnosis of a serious illness, starting therapies, losing life partners—journeys that make up the big journey. Each stage in life is a journey.

I am grateful to those who were sincere in sharing their life stories that became part of this book. I am greatly indebted to my children, Tiji and Timmy, who have taken time from their busy professions to proofread and correct spelling mistakes and grammatical errors. If you read excellently structured sentences in this book, they were probably edited by one of them.

The book would not have been possible without Evangeline, my wife and beloved fellow traveler on my life's journey. I am thankful for her insight in designing the cover and selecting the cover picture. I am indebted to my grandparents and parents, who ingrained in me a deep-rooted faith. I am also thankful for several mentors, teachers, and acquaintances who supported me with great ideas and suggestions.

Mathew Philip

# INTRODUCTION

In November 2018, a young American made a doomed mission to North Sentinel Island, a speck in the Bay of Bengal, with the dream of spreading Christianity to a people who had lived in seclusion for thousands of years. No outsiders knew their language or where they had come from. We don't even know what they call themselves—definitely not the Sentinelese as some people do. The island is home to perhaps the most isolated people on earth; they number about fifty.

Ever since he had been a boy, John Chau, an evangelical missionary, dreamed of following a call of spreading Christianity to the people on North Sentinel. The tribespeople shot him with arrows and killed him; his body was buried in the sand. Some have called him naïve, delusional, and reckless while others considered his journey to be the calling of someone who was fortunate to have lived in luxury but hoped to reach a tribal group and bring them to a better standard of life. The survival of a few dozen groups of hunter-gatherers living in complete isolation may seem unfair and unjust. Many experts say they may not survive undisturbed for much longer.

In 1956, five missionaries were killed while participating in a similar effort called Operation Auca, an attempt to evangelize the Huaorani people of Ecuador. Since then, continued and organized efforts of several groups have proven that transformation is possible and rehabilitation can be successful. From a dwindling six hundred members in 1958, the tribe has grown to two thousand.

Not long ago, on January 23, 1999, Graham Staines, a missionary who translated the Bible for the Ho tribes in the northeastern hills of India along with his two sons, Philip and Timothy, was burned to death by a gang of religious fundamentalists while sleeping in his station wagon at Manoharpur in Odisha, India.

Then there are those who like Hudson Taylor followed a call to China, and William Carey went to India under dangerous and risky circumstances. All of these heroes followed their calls and started journeys that eventually impacted the world and history. We all know that the effects of their work brought the good news of the love of Jesus Christ to various people and blessings to the lands they traveled to. The world will forever be thankful to them for choosing to undertake those journeys.

CHAPTER I

# The Journey Starts with a Call

Each call for a journey is a call to an adventure, an exploration of unknown territory. This involves a certain amount of risk, uncertainty, and unexpected experiences. The Bible is full of stories of calls to adventure. God called Abraham, Moses, David, and many others to adventure. Abraham accepted the call and started a journey to a place he did not know. Moses left Pharaoh's palace for a new life with the people of God. In Hebrews 11:25–19, we read, "By faith Moses, when he had grown up, refused to be known as the son of Pharaoh's daughter." Moses accepted the call to lead the people of Israel from their bondage on a journey through the desert for forty years. David took up the call from God while he was a shepherd boy not knowing that he would become Israel's greatest king. Jesus called fishermen, who later changed the history of the world after accepting and following their calls. All of them had one thing in common—they went on journeys that were not easy but were challenging.

A journey follows a call or a revelation. A star appeared in the east—that was a revelation to the wise men who followed the star on a long and challenging journey. The star of Bethlehem, or Christmas star, appears only in the nativity story in the gospel of Matthew, where "wise men from the East" (commonly known as the Magi) were inspired by the star to travel west. This calling led them to the palace of King Herod and from there to Jesus, where they worshipped Him and gave Him gifts.

Many Christians believe the star was a miraculous sign to mark the birth of the Christ, the Messiah. Some theologians claimed that the star fulfilled a prophecy, but some modern scholars do not consider that to have been a historical event but just fiction. In the *US News and World Report* (December 20, 1999), a British astrophysicist argued that the Bethlehem star was indeed a real star that can still be seen by telescopes today. At the time of Jesus's birth, it was a bright nova. He argued that ancient astrologers would have found the nova significant because of where and when it appeared—"during a triple conjunction of Jupiter and Saturn in the constellation of Pisces." According to this researcher, the conjunctions would have told the Magi to await news from Judea and, possibly, to expect the imminent birth of the "Messiah."

I want to note a few things here. First, these events took place after Jesus's birth. Second, this was in the days of King Herod the Great. Third, the Magi already arrived at Jerusalem when Matthew described it. They were not following a star from east to west as we are used to hearing in stories and songs—"Westward leading still proceeding" makes us think that the star was going ahead from east to west. We all know stars don't travel; they remain where they are.

Fourth, the Magi came from east of Jerusalem, probably from the vicinity of Babylon, Arabia, or Persia. And last, they knew they were looking for the newborn king of the Jews, but the exact location eluded them.

A closer reading of Matthew 2:9 indicates the star appeared before the wise men started and reappeared over Bethlehem, just about six miles south of Jerusalem, after they got lost. When the wise men said, "We saw his star in the east," they didn't mean, "We saw his star while we were in the east." The Greek text here says the star was *en anatole*, meaning they saw his star rising in the east.

There is still even now a star rising in the east, in the west, in the south, and in the north. How many today would look for it? How many would be interested in the star of Bethlehem? It comes in the form of God's Word, people, and events. In the midst of darkness, where light is needed, God sends a star. In the midst of war and bloodshed, God has a star shining to guide us to the source of peace. In the midst of our personal struggles, sickness, broken relationships, and lack of security, there is the shining star of Bethlehem that will guide us to the Prince of Peace.

The wise men followed their thirst to experience God rather than follow a moving star. They studied the star because they were wise. They had a thirst to ponder God and eternity. They were astrologers who studied the planets. They had seen an unusual new star, and they knew it told of the birth of a special king for the Jewish people. The message here is that the Gentiles had seen the sign of the birth of the Son of God while the religious leaders, scholars, and Herod in Jerusalem missed the Messiah entirely!

The star is an invitation or a call to set out on a journey. All people can see the star, but only the wise will pursue its message. The world can see any star in the sky, but not all stars lead to God. In fact, there is only one star that led them to Jesus. Many may be curious but don't seek to understand, and others do not care; it is for the wise to follow the message of the signs.

It was a sign that the prophets and the forefathers told thousands of years ago—that a Savior would be born. It had been foretold since the fall of Adam. This was foretold by ancient Eastern religions as well as Western religions. We read the scripture daily but often miss God's message. Many people know a lot about Jesus, but they do not know who He is. It is personal knowledge that leads us to worship Him. It is about knowing Jesus and being known by Him. It is a knowledge that leads us to worship Him as Lord. The star of the east was a message of salvation to the Gentiles.

God's loving calls reach to the farthest corners of the earth. Dante spoke of "the love that moves the stars." There are no measures God will not try and no group He cannot reach. His call is to ordinary people and wise men—old and young, men and women. There are signs to seek all around us. The star is a sign of God seeking all in this world, and anyone who responds and believes will be saved. Jesus said in John 3:14, "Just as Moses lifted up the snake in the wilderness, so the Son of Man must be lifted up that everyone who believes may have eternal life in him." When people started perishing due to snake bites, God asked Moses to lift up a brass serpent so people looking at it would not die. There stands a pole—the cross raised up on the hill of Calvary—that those who look up to and go to will be saved by; they will know the presence of God in their lives. God provided a way of redemption, pointing to the only Son of God, who would be sacrificed. Those who first received it died without the sight.

After the days of Enoch, the promise was repeated through patriarchs and prophets, and that kept the hope of His appearing alive; Daniel's prophecy revealed the time of His advent. Century after century passed, and the voices of the prophets ceased. With longing eyes, they looked for the coming of the deliverer, when the darkness would be dispelled and the mystery of the future would be made plain.

But like the stars in the vast circuit of their appointed path, God's purposes know no haste and no delay. So in heaven's council, the hour for the coming of Christ had been determined. When the great clock of time pointed to that hour, Jesus was born in Bethlehem. "But when the set time had fully come, God sent his Son, born of a woman" (Galatians 4:4). He came to spend His time with us.

There are stars all around us. Recently, Handel's *Messiah* was performed in China in the Forbidden City Concert Hall in Beijing after it had been banned for several decades. The choir assembled by a local Christian conductor sang to a packed house. A news reporter wrote, "There wasn't a dry eye among the thousands assembled as they all stood for the 'Hallelujah' chorus."

As hostility to Christianity and the gospel grows in the West, there is revival happening in India, China, and Indonesia in the East. If the current rate of growth holds, by 2030, there will be more Christians in China—about 295 million—than in any other nation on earth. At universities in China, Christianity is growing at a faster rate than ever.

The Liushi Church in China opened in 2013 in the small Liushi Township, Yueqing District of Wenzhou, in Zhejiang Province. According to news reports, it is now China's largest church with seating for 5,000. It is another star in the East; it has more than twice as many seats as

Westminster Abbey does, and its 206-foot crucifix can be seen for miles. A local resident noted that it was a miracle that such a small town was able to build such a grand church. The £8 million (US $ 10 million) building is also one of the most visible symbols of Communist China's breakneck conversion during which thousands of worshippers will flock to pledge their allegiance not to the Communist party but to the cross. "It is a wonderful thing to be a follower of Jesus Christ. It gives us great confidence," beamed Jin Hongxin, a member. "If everyone in China believed in Jesus then we would have no more need for police stations. There would be no more bad people and therefore no more crime," she added. A recent study found that online searches for "Christian Congregation" and "Jesus" far outnumbered those for "Communist Party" and "Xi Jinping," China's president. It is a testament to the fact that neither Marx nor Mao gets the last word in China—the Messiah does.

We are all stars of the East that others may follow. God wants us to shine like stars so the world can follow Christ. The September 1993 issue of *Global Prayer Digest* tells the story of Jonah, a seventy-three-year-old Chinese evangelist who since 1976 has traveled around the People's Republic spreading the good news about Jesus Christ.

> His days are full, and his energy unflagging. In one weekend Jonah may bicycle nine hours, spend 40 hours on a hard railway seat and eight hours on a bumpy bus just to bring the message

of Jesus Christ to people in remote villages, or to urban churches with 5,000 members, or to young soldiers. The schedule is grueling, but 73-year-old Jonah says, "Rest is for the next world."(Global Prayer Digest September 1993).

He is a star in the East pointing people to Jesus. Recently, the Communist Party has been alarmed, and President Xi Jinping ordered Chinese Christians to replace pictures of Jesus with pictures of himself or lose benefits from the Poverty Relief Quota, assistance provided to poor people.

Jerusalem is shining as a star in the East. Several countries have recognized Jerusalem as the capital of Israel. You wouldn't need to be warned in a dream. Wherever you sit, stand, walk, or lie down, there is going to be someone to your west, and there will always be someone to your east. You are the shining Bethlehem star for them.

We are here today to point them to Christ. Jesus is coming again, and the star has risen in the east, west, north, and south. "You shall be witnesses to Me in Jerusalem, and in all Judea and Samaria, and to the end of the earth" (Acts 1:8). Jesus is not a stranger to any culture, race, or geographical location. Whatever the exact mechanism, the fact that the star led the Magi to Christ is evidence that the star was uniquely designed and made by God for a very special purpose. God can use extraordinary means for extraordinary purposes. Certainly, the birth of our Lord was deserving of honor in the heavens. It is fitting that God used a celestial object to announce the birth of Christ since "the heavens declare the glory of God" (Psalm 19:1).

Paul preached the gospel in Greece, where he saw many idols. One temple there had been dedicated "To the unknown god." He did not quote the Bible even once in his sermon in Athens; the people there would not have had any point of reference in regard to Hebrew scriptures. Paul preached about the God they worshipped without knowing—God revealed in Jesus Christ to all cultures, races, and ethnicities. As theologian Timothy Tennent stated, "Christ does not arrive in any culture as a stranger"[1.] God has provided pathways in every culture around the world where culture and Christ intersect. As Paul said, "The god of this age has blinded the minds of unbelievers, so that they cannot see the light of the gospel that displays the glory of Christ, who is the image of God" (2 Corinthians 4:4). The precious goes unnoticed in the heap of the worthless, and many miss the call.

Today, many churches have created an artificial environment that goes beyond the simplicity of Christian faith. They have their own languages and customs, and in many cases, those who enter those churches encounter culture shock. If we are causing our visitors to experience culture shock, we are failing our mission. If we cannot hear

---

[1] Timothy C. Tennent, *Theology in the Context of World Christianity: How the Global Church Is Influencing the Way We Think about and Discuss Theology*, (Grand Rapids, Michigan: Zondervan, 2007), 69.

the cry in the hearts of the people in the community and cannot relate to their daily struggles, we will not be able to preach the gospel of Christ in any impactful way. A church that my wife and I attended for some time had decided to close its doors. The church has a rich history dating to the 1950s; it has grown into a large congregation with over 300 members at its peak in the 1970s. The congregation's fear of running out of money and the church being closed or the fear of losing control paralyzed growth. Change is inevitable, and it must happen sooner than later.

Many modern theologians seem to reconstruct theology into a "new" theology more reflective of the latest cultural trends. Modern studies of Jesus focus mostly on His earthly life based on His location and the political and pragmatic usefulness of His teachings. Their studies do not include the doctrine of the Trinity, eternal sonship, or incarnation and thus miss the message of His birth. He is the Son derived from the Father but not after the manner of generation; unlike our parent-child relationships in which children later become parents themselves, God the Father has always been a father and God the Son has always been a son. Jesus, the Son of God, was eternally begotten from the Father, so there is nothing chronological in this designation, nothing to suggest a second-order existence. It is an identification grounded in a relationship. He is God the Son, a simple and undivided part of the Trinity who deserves all glory, honor, and worship.

But God lovingly warns us that we need to take a new route as the wise men did: "They left for their own country by another road" (Matthew 2:12). They took a different highway, but I imagine Matthew winking a little and hoping we would notice his subtle clue about what life was like once we had met Jesus. Nothing is the same; we find ourselves going another way.

T. S. Eliot ended his poem, "Journey of the Magi" imagining the thoughts of the Magi: "We returned to our places ... but no longer at ease here, in the old dispensation, with an alien people clutching their gods." Jesus does not make our lives more comfortable; He doesn't help us fit in and succeed. A strange, unfamiliar road is now our path. But the road is going somewhere. "You are the light of the world. A city that is set on a hill cannot be hidden. Nor do they light a lamp and put it under a basket, but on a lampstand, and it gives light to all who are in the house. Let your light so shine before men, that they may see your good works and glorify your Father in heaven" (Matthew 5:14–16).

God revealed Himself in His Son, Jesus, as the light of the world. Go and join our voices with angels and saints, those who have gone before us, and the generations that will follow to be a beacon of love, peace, and justice with compassion for one another and in witness to the world.

CHAPTER 2

# The Potential in the Unexpected

M y wife takes care of plants. In the several places we have lived in our years of marriage, she has tended whatever was available; she has rescued a flowerbed from invasive lilies of the valley. We have one plant that is almost thirty years old. She does not throw away any plants even including those I think are dying. When we go on vacation, she makes sure that our son or a neighbor waters her plants in the house.

When we would move to a new home, I would suggest that she tossed some of the dying ones, but she would find a small space in the kitchen or family room, just the right size for the ugly pot, and bring it to our new home. If that plant did indeed die, nothing would be lost. And on a couple of occasions, I saw my assumptions were wrong. As months passed, one leaf and then another and another appeared. With warm sunshine and an occasional drink of water, I saw little plants begin to thrive.

Every time I look at the now-flourishing plants, I am reminded of how easily I make judgments about everything's potential—from plants to people. I think, *Oh, she'll never amount to anything,* or *Look at all his tattoos!* or *What chance does he have coming from a home like that?* or *She shouldn't hire him—he's done time in prison.* God looks at people's hearts, not their outward appearances or circumstances.

Jesus called fishermen to take up a new career path, to go on an adventure. The call was not just to be followers; it was to take up the cross and deliver the gospel to the ends of the world. That required full commitment and dedication. Our calls require us to open our lives from an inward-looking perspective to an outward-looking vision. All of us face moments—in some cases many moments— that challenge our center of gravity or focus and want to shift it from a story of self to one that will mean something in a larger context. If you dug into a fisherman's personality profile, I'm guessing you might not find a college degree or proven leadership abilities. Many are probably introverts. Jesus found three fishermen when they were casting their nets. They weren't teaching others how to cast nets; they were getting their hands dirty casting their own nets, doing the work themselves. These were the men He chose to carry out

His vision of sharing the gospel. They were quiet guys who worked hard with their hands and got the job done in less-than-ideal conditions. They were used to weathering storms. They were persistent and patient, and they were hardworking and action-oriented. They never knew what a new day was going to be like. They took their chances every day. They were never distracted by the success or the failure of the previous day; they focused on the present day and put their hopes in the next day.

In John 21, we read about how after the resurrection, Peter and some other disciples went back to their fishing business but weren't succeeding; they didn't catch anything. The resurrected Jesus appeared to them and asked, "Friends, haven't you any fish?" "No," they answered. He said, "Throw your net on the right side of the boat and you will find some." When they did, they were unable to haul the net in because of the large number of fish. Peter turned and saw that the "disciple whom Jesus loved" was following them. (This was the one who had leaned back against Jesus at the supper and asked Him, "Lord, who is going to betray you?") When Peter saw him, he asked, "Lord, what about him?" Because of this, the rumor spread among the believers that this disciple would not die. But Jesus did not say that he would not die; he only said, "If I want him to remain alive until I return, what is that to you? You follow me" (John 21:20–23).

Jesus called Peter to establish the church. He preached a short message, and 3,000 souls were saved, and later, 5,000 more were saved. Thomas went to Asia, and Paul preached the gospel to the Gentiles in Europe and Asia. God used the great missionaries including John and Charles Wesley, D. L. Moody, Charles Spurgeon, Billy Graham, and many others. All of them had different traits and talents, but God used them all. He is calling you and me today. Are you willing to follow Him? Or do you just want to be a spectator on the sidelines?

Jesus taught the parable of the laborers in the vineyard in Matthew 21:1–16. The owner of the vineyard hired laborers at different times of the day but paid them all the same wage for their work at the end of the day. Jesus was saying that all who labored for the sake of the kingdom of God would receive the same reward no matter when they started their labors—whether early or late in life. Some people who labor for Jesus would be happier if they received more than those who come in for the last few hours, so to speak, but it's not for them to claim they've done more and thus deserve more; it's not for them to narrow the field.

At a deeper level, we are all those eleventh-hour workers, but we are all nonetheless honored guests in God's kingdom. We should not worry about who started work at sunrise and who got to work only at four in the afternoon; God calls us all on His terms, wages, and position. Some might think He does not pay fair wages, but He does supply all his workers' needs. Believe me, I would rather have God's grace than fairness.

I read about a pastor in northern India who struggled with stuttering his entire life. He was teased and harassed as a boy. But as a young man he heard God calling him to fish for people by becoming a preacher. This seemed to be an impossible calling; nevertheless he said, "Here I am, Lord." He went to school and ultimately became a preacher. He continued to stutter his entire life, but an interesting thing happened to him when he would stand in the pulpit to preach: his stuttering went away, and instead he delivered, with power and eloquence, the message of Christ. God used him to build a church with many thousands of people in a low-income community. The church included former prostitutes and drug dealers worshiping side-by-side with business leaders and educators. It was one of the most diverse and dynamic congregations.

Our calling is an invitation to greater opportunities in spite of the obstacles we face. Our task is to go out from this place and be witnesses. Each of us has at least one story to share in small decisions and in overwhelming decisions alike to follow a journey. God has promised to be with us in all those decisions. I think of Janie, Barbara, Ed, Paul, John, and many others I came to know in life and those who are challenged to make journeys to unknown territories. They waited patiently through all their ordeals; they prepared themselves for chemotherapy, radiation, and surgery, and they think of how they passed through each territory with faith and patience and how God equipped them to cross that territory.

One of the ways God has helped them is through their community of faith by prayers and visits. They know the love of God through the people of God. Others of us have been challenged to stand up for what we believe in our work, at home, or in our relationships, finances, or health. We remember what Rosa Parks, Mahatma Gandhi, and Nelson Mandela stood up for in all the journeys they endured. We must remember that the God of Abraham, Moses, and Joshua is with us through the power of Jesus's resurrection. Let us thank God for helping us cross those rivers of life, and let us join hands and help others cross as well. God often calls us to chart unknown territory as we follow Him. Obeying His commands to forgive, to give away our treasures, and to give up things that provide security and pleasure often leave us in the scary territory of unknown outcomes.

Recently, a student shared his story with me. He was disappointed that he did not have the grades to get into the college he wanted. He said, "I have always been very confident in my abilities. Because my plans were not working out, I wondered if God still cared about me. But the Lord wisely led me another way: I was able to study in another college that enabled me to commute from home. That in turn gave me the opportunity to stay with my parents and attend their church. The opportunity helped to deepen my relationship with my family and others and allowed me to appreciate what is special in each one of them. Now, I thank God for not answering my prayer in the way that I had wanted. Not being able to fulfill my will at that time put me into better circumstances. I have learned the power in using the gifts and talents God has given each of us to help others as much as we can."

# CHAPTER 3

# Loneliness on the Journey

I heard a mother of five saying to her daughter, who had come back from college on vacation after a year of study, "I felt so lonely without you." You may have several people at home and friends at work. You may have the best fellowship at church, but you still feel lonely when you miss the presence of someone you love. There is that void of loneliness in your life only that person can fill. It does not matter how old you are or what kind of work you do; loneliness can be real to anyone. The loneliness children feel is real. Some psychologists say that the main reason infants cry during their first three months is loneliness. Since they so often stop crying when they are cuddled, it seems their cries are not likely from physical pain but from loneliness and due to a need to be embraced.

Youth and middle-aged people are not immune to loneliness. A unique loneliness sets in at times on our journeys. Dreams are built and tested during youth, and the pain of shattered dreams affects us during midlife. And loneliness is very real in old age. The only way to be entirely free from loneliness is to be oblivious to our surroundings, oblivious to animals and human beings and even to God.

Modern life has many blessings including the company of social media and virtual friends and user groups, but loneliness seems to be increasing. Vance Havner pointed out that "no generation has had more amusements and entertainments than modern Americans, but there have never been more lonely people." We live in a crowded society but go through the elevator experience—there are people around us and physically close, but no one talks to others. At each floor, people get off and go their own ways. A Gallop poll said that four out of ten Americans admit to frequent feelings of intense loneliness. Mother Teresa said, "Loneliness is the greatest form of poverty."

All great heroes of the Bible have lamented their loneliness. David was alone in the caves and jungles when he wrote many psalms. Jacob was alone in his tent when he was tested. Elijah was alone by the brook. Job was lonely even when he was surrounded by friends. Moses was alone on the backside of that mountain where God met him. Joseph was alone in the pit. Jesus was alone in the agony of Gethsemane and Calvary. The psalmist who wrote Psalm 102:6–7, a prayer of the afflicted, was experiencing loneliness.

> I resemble a pelican of the wilderness
> (thirsty and tired); I have become like
> an owl of the desert (I lie awake at
> night), I have become like a lonely bird
> on a housetop (loneliness). I looked on
> my right hand, and beheld, but there
> was no man that would know me.

We all have experienced when we find that friends seem to turn their faces from us as if we have committed a crime or something.

A woman from Oklahoma wrote in a blog,

> For many months, my six children
> and I were homeless and living in
> our rundown car. We got most of our
> food out of dumpsters and washed
> up in gas station bathrooms. Each
> day we fought to survive. Family and
> friends turned away from us as if we
> had committed a crime. Most people
> who saw us living in the car pretended
> they had not seen us. I felt invisible.
> Everything we owned had been sold in
> a garage sale as I tried to avoid being
> homeless. All that was left were some
> clothes, blankets, some dishes, and
> my Bible. At night, while the children
> slept, I cried, not knowing what to do. I
> prayed, telling God that I was ready to
> give up. One night I opened my Bible
> seeking strength and found the verse
> quoted above. I stared at the words,
> then read them over and over again,
> seeing the meaning and the power
> behind them. This verse assured me
> that no matter what hardships we face,
> no matter what obstacles life throws

at us, God, through Christ, has given
us the strength to overcome them.
From time to time, we all face events
that knock us down. They seem too
powerful for us to conquer until we
remember that we are in God's hands
at all times. With the help of God and
some loving people God sent to us, my
family escaped having to live in the car.
I know now that we face nothing alone
because through Christ, we fight no
battle without God's help.

The truth is that none of us needs to make this journey alone.

Dr. Norman Vincent Peale, a pastor and author of *The Power of Positive Thinking*, was passing through an airport. The gate agent knew him and knew that he often traveled with his wife; he said to Peale, "I see you're traveling alone today, Dr. Peale." He responded, "Yes, I'm traveling alone today." As he moved on, the agent said, "You don't travel alone." Dr. Peale replied, "Neither do you."

There is One who will be everywhere with us even to eternity. Loneliness is a tutor; it teaches us to make that friendship continuous and strong, so strong that we will sing, "On life's pathway, I am never lonely." If we ever find ourselves lonely, we should remember that we are receiving private tutoring to experience that friendship with the eternal One.

The absence of someone we miss causes us to feel lonely, and we realize we are not completely self-sufficient. Sometimes, we suppress our loneliness because we do not want others to know, but when we do that, we kill a part of ourselves. Recognizing and acknowledging our feelings of loneliness are important. We see that God recognized our need for fellowship even at Creation. Looking at Adam, God sensed and addressed the problem; He said, "It is not good that he should be alone" (Genesis 2:18) and created Eve. We are singular enough that we need some solitude but incomplete enough and similar enough that we need one another.

Mary and Martha expressed their loneliness to Jesus: "If only you had been here, our brother would not have died." They felt abandoned and desperate without His presence. With the death of their only loving brother, they felt lost and helpless. "If only you had been here …" I think about the past many times and wonder, "If only …" But Jesus wanted to let them know that His love was deeper than "if only." He wanted them to know He was and would always be with them no matter what happened. God's love is much deeper and wider than any narrow depravity we find ourselves in on the journey. Jesus can make a difference in our lives if we feel helpless.

Terry Anderson was a war correspondent and reporter who was kidnapped in Beirut on March 16, 1985, and was imprisoned for about seven years till he was released in December 1991. In his book *Den of Lions*, he wrote his harrowing and poignant story of his loneliness in captivity. He was driven around blindfolded and tied to a bed for several days. He told someone walking by, "Hey mister, don't do this to me! I'm a human. I'm going crazy."

The next day, someone took off his blindfold, and he saw a Bible on his bed. He was so happy to be able to read it. He remembered Paul in prison. He thought about his family; he didn't know his brother and father had died while he was there. He concluded, "The captivity has changed me to become a fearless person, gave me a faith that is fearless." Loneliness is a private tutor that trains you in becoming fearless in your journey ahead.

William Cowper (1731–1800) wrote the hymns "God Moves in a Mysterious Way" and "There Is a Fountain Filled with Blood." He suffered frequently from extreme loneliness that often led to almost depression. One cold and snowy night, he found himself depressed and lonely. He decided to commit suicide by jumping into the River Thames. He called a cab and told the driver to take him to the river. However, thick fog came down and prevented them from finding the river. (Another version of the story has the driver getting lost deliberately.) After driving around for a while, the cab driver gave up; he stopped and let Cowper out. To Cowper's surprise, he found himself on his own doorstep. Cowper realized that even in our blackest moments, God watches over us in mysterious ways. His beautiful hymn goes like this.

> Ye fearful saints, fresh courage take;
> The clouds ye so much dread

Are big with mercy and shall break
In blessings on your head.

I don't think he would have written with such faith and insight had he not struggled with loneliness and found a deeper friendship with God.

Our situations of loneliness are private tutors we don't have to pay. They teach us to find a better friendship with God. We can turn our lonely places into our blessed classrooms. The ultimate relationship for us human beings is beyond our situations, our natures, our spouses, children, and others. It is the love of Jesus that comprehends all understanding. Paul prayed for the Ephesians in his letter to the Ephesians 3:18 "to grasp how wide and long and high and deep is the love of Christ." We may not like it, and we may not understand it, but when we find ourselves in a lonely place where we have no one and nothing but God, He is more than sufficient—He is more than enough, and He will never leave us or forsake us (Hebrews 13:5). He is a faithful friend and a very present help in trouble. Psalm 46:1 tells us that God is the only friend who will always be with us. We sing the beautiful hymn,

What a friend we have in Jesus ...
Do thy friends despise forsake you,
take it to the Lord in prayer.
In his arms He will take and shield thee.
Thou wilt find a solace there.

The love of Jesus far exceeds any other love. His presence is constantly with us.

# CHAPTER 4

# Table in the Wilderness

The need for food becomes real on our journeys. The psalmist asked, "Can God furnish a table in the wilderness?" (Psalm 78:19). Our trust in a God, who provides us with abundant blessings and provision, makes our journeys joyful. God becomes the chef through the journey who prepares the table at any time and in any circumstance.

The people of Israel were led through the wilderness in their journey to the Promised Land. Some accounts estimate that there were anywhere from 2 to 5 million people. Two million people would require two trains one and a half miles long filled with food, but God gave them manna six days a week for forty years. It would take a train 1,800 miles long to supply water for that many people for forty years; that train would stretch from coast to coast in the United States. But God provided water from a rock, about 11 million gallons per day!

But then God's people said they were tired of manna; they wanted meat. So God sent a strong east wind, and quail got caught up in it; they were six feet deep around the camp. He who gathered the least gathered 105 bushels of quail, 6,700 quail each; that was $20 billion worth of quail. The Bible says they ate it for thirty days until it came out their noses. Can you imagine what they did with the feathers?

When God is the chef, food becomes plentiful.

Christian evangelist George Muller founded several orphanages that took care of over 10,000 children during his life. One night, Muller was informed that the supply of food was gone at one of the houses. The next morning, he joined the children for breakfast. There were bowls, plates, and glasses in front of each of the several hundred children, but all were empty. Muller asked the children to bow their heads as he prayed. His words included "Father, we thank Thee for what Thou art going to give us to eat." After he ended the prayer, there was a knock at the door. A baker stood there and said, "I couldn't sleep last night. I felt that you didn't have any bread and that the Lord wanted me to send you some, so I got up at two this morning and baked some fresh bread for you." Muller thanked the baker and said a prayer of thanksgiving to God.

Later that day, another miracle happened. A milkman

came by and said his milk cart had broken down in front of the home. The milk had to be unloaded and he wanted to give it to the home for the children. "Would you take it?" he asked. God's supply is immeasurable and timely.

A boy and mother were at the checkout counter at a grocery store. There was a large bowl of candies at the counter and a sign that read, Free—Take a Handful. The boy looked at the bowl, and the cashier told him to take a handful for free, but the boy didn't want to do it. Finally, the cashier grabbed a handful of candy and gave it to him. On their way out, the mother asked him why he hadn't grabbed the candy himself. He said, "The cashier has bigger hands than mine." When we allow God to give us, He will give us in good measure.

The book of Ruth is about two women who took risky and challenging journeys to foreign lands. During a famine, an Israelite family from Bethlehem—Elimelech, his wife Naomi, and their sons Mahlon and Chilion—immigrated to the nearby country of Moab. Elimelech died, and the sons married two Moabite women: Mahlon married Ruth and Chilion married Orpah. After about ten years, Naomi's two sons died in Moab (Ruth 1:4). Naomi decided to return to Bethlehem. She told her daughters-in-law to return to their own mothers and remarry. Orpah reluctantly left, but Ruth replied,

> Don't urge me to leave you or to turn
> back from you. Where you go I will go,

and where you stay I will stay. Your
people will be my people and your God
my God. Where you die I will die, and
there I will be buried. May the Lord
deal with me, be it ever so severely,
if even death separates you and me.
(Ruth 1:16–17)

When she came back to Bethlehem, she had nobody to turn to for help. Naomi told her neighbors not to call her Naomi but to call her Mara, which means "bitter." She was caught up in her own little pity party. I am sure there are at least one or two people you know who are always caught up in pity parties. They will talk about their arthritis or their bills. They will talk about how somebody just did them wrong. And it's the same story all the time. Naomi was bitter, and she blamed everything on God. She talked of how she had left home full but returned home empty. She described how God had testified against her and afflicted her.

Notice that Ruth never complained; she was a good friend to Naomi. She wasn't expecting anything in return; she just wanted to help. When they arrived in Bethlehem, Ruth decided to work in the fields following the harvesters and picking up barley they had dropped. The owner of the field came by to greet the harvesters and noticed Ruth in the field. He asked one of the harvesters who she was and was told, "She came back from Moab with Naomi—that's all we know." Lucky for Ruth, the owner of the field was Boaz, a kind man who believed in God. He had also been related to Elimelech, Naomi's late husband.

Boaz told Ruth, "Don't go work in any other field. Stay here with the other servant girls. I will make sure you are safe. Whenever you are thirsty, get a drink from the water jars."

When Ruth heard that, she bowed to Boaz and asked, "Why are you being so nice to me? I'm not even from here."

Boaz replied, "I know what you've done for Naomi. You left your family and moved to a place you've never been. May the Lord reward you for your kindness."

Ruth thanked Boaz and continued with her work in the hot sun. Boaz even ordered his workers to drop extra barley so Ruth could have more for herself. Ruth took all the barley home and shared it with Naomi. Eventually, Ruth married Boaz, and everyone was very happy and she became part of the genealogy of Jesus (Matthew 1).

Even in the midst of some of your most trying times, even when it seems there is no hope for tomorrow, if you keep on trusting in the Lord and look for God's blessing, He will always give you a harvest.

Ben Carpenter has muscular dystrophy; he gets around in an electric wheelchair. One day as he was crossing an intersection, the light changed and a trailer truck caught the handles of Ben's wheelchair in its grille. Unaware, the driver started down the road, and before long, Ben was being pushed along at fifty miles per hour. Soon, the rubber on the wheelchair's tires began to burn off. Passersby saw the bizarre sight and called 911. When the truck driver pulled over, he was astonished to see what was attached to his truck's grille. Ben had had a big scare but escaped without injury. His journey in a wheelchair stuck to that grille was uncommon and scary. Ben wrote, "Such journeys make us look to the future and give us a hopeful and promising eagerness to go forward."

# CHAPTER 5

# Highway in the Desert

For those of us who drive regularly, highways are places of frequent aggravation—traffic, accidents, people driving without rules or directions, on and on. I sometimes ask my wife to drive if I have to speak at a meeting or lead a seminar so that I won't be stressed out when I get there.

The highways always seem to be under construction one direction or the other; at least that's how it seems. Desert highways are even more challenging; one in Jordan is even called the Desert Highway. You need to keep a good lookout in case a donkey, goat, or camel is wandering across. Someone who recently drove that highway was misled by the directions posted because some were in English and Arabic while others were in Arabic only. So he stopped and told a policeman about his problem. The policeman said, "The important signs are in English and Arabic. When you see a sign in Arabic alone, it means you don't need to take any notice of it, it is not for you."

China completed the world's longest desert highway in 2016; it's over 1,500 miles and goes mostly through remote areas such as the Gobi Desert. A similar highway in the US—Route 50—runs from California to Maryland, over 3,000 miles, through mostly rural desert and mountains in the West. A stretch that runs through Nevada is called the Desert Road and is referred to as the loneliest road in America.

Desert highways are not places of fun; they are sometimes marked with danger and fear. In the past, bands of robbers roamed deserts making them unsafe places. Deserts are inhospitable and parched. Deserts are the locations for many biblical stories that set adversity against the power of God's provision. Abraham was led through the wilderness, Moses fasted for forty days in the wilderness, the prophet Elijah was lonely in the wilderness, and David sang many songs while exiled in the wilderness. Jesus was tested in the wilderness. Deserts are where we experience God's way to redemption.

Deserts for us might not be filled with lots of sand and no water, but I bet there are times in all our lives that we have felt we were in a desert. We felt that our spirituality was dried up, and we wanted the living water to revive our souls. These deserts might not be wildernesses or filled with sand, but they are frightening places nonetheless. I think about those who are in the wilderness of trying to make ends meet; they are living from paycheck to paycheck and making do with meager resources as they try to climb out of debt. I think about how desert-like it can feel when people we know have been diagnosed with illnesses and we don't know how to support them. That can feel very much like a wilderness. We feel grief when we are left alone isolated and surrounded by a wilderness of memories. We feel we are in a desert that is no longer in bloom.

In Mark 1:2–3, we read, "As it is written in the prophet Isaiah, 'See, I am sending my messenger ahead of you, who will prepare your way; the voice of one crying out in the wilderness: "Prepare the way of the Lord, make his paths straight." A voice in the wilderness calls for every valley to be raised and every mountain and hill made low. The rough ground becomes level and the rugged places are made plain.

John the Baptist appeared "as the voice in the wilderness" (John 1:23); he proclaimed the baptism of repentance for the forgiveness of sins. He was clothed with camel's hair, had a leather belt around his waist, and ate locusts and wild honey. The amazing thing is that even in desert places, God establishes highways, holy ways, so those who cannot see a way out can regain hope and those who are paralyzed by depression and anxiety can leap for joy again. Those who thirst for justice might drink from the pool of living water. This highway that is coming to the desert places is the flesh of

God incarnate. The way in the desert will become a highway to bring God's grace to the world in need.

Into our lives and into our desert places, Jesus comes to us in the middle of our weakness and says, "I am here with you. You are not alone." We remember that God is with us—Emmanuel—each time we gather as believers; we see a highway leading to God's grace. God gives us promise and hope; He "strengthens the weak hands, and makes firm feeble knees, says to those who are of a fearful heart, do not fear! Here is your God, He will come and save you!" God creates highways that lead us to redemption even in the most troubling experiences.

But the road continues. Where do we go from here? Church is not an institution but a road that has been paved by thousands and thousands of Christians through history. This highway takes the living presence of God to parched and lonely lands. This highway springs up living water to thirsty souls and gives directions to those who are lost or without goals in life. One soul at a time, one community at a time, we continue to hear the whisper of God and step forward as new paving stones for God's highway ready to live our moments in God's history as lives that count.

In Isaiah's day, the people saw this hope and highway as exiled prisoners returned from Babylon to the holy city of Jerusalem. In Jesus's day, they saw this highway be born in a manger, teach and heal in the countryside, and stand with them in the locked room after His crucifixion to leave them with His peace.

Today, we see God's highway of grace take shape in our hands each time we share our resources, volunteer our time, or help our neighbors in need. We become the highway in the desert making a way for God's grace to enter our world. As the body of Christ, we have a lot of work to do to build that highway for God's grace. Many live today without hope and in fear and anxiety, and it's our job to help them see the highway of God's love that comes to them in their desert places.

As Christians, we are invited to prepare a way in the world so all might experience the highway of Christ. And so, maybe this year is a good year to think about who needs to experience the highway, whose feeble faith needs to be reassured this year by the good news of a Savior who comes very near to them.

Maybe this is the year you invite them to church so they can experience the true wonder of this season and the true gift of Emmanuel; they will see God drawing near to them, as near as our hands, doing God's work. Each bit of good we do establishes a highway for God to transform the desert. We as disciples stand as signs along God's highway pointing the way to the manger, the cross, the table, and the bath. We show people the holy way to transformation, forgiveness, resurrection, a new life, a way out of the desert.

We are the new highway of God's grace transforming others' lives as we share the good news of God through our words and deeds in Jesus's name.

CHAPTER 6

# And Then the Manna Stopped Falling

One of the secrets to enjoying the journey is counting our blessings along the way. A group of elementary school students were asked to write down the Seven Wonders of the World, and they mentioned the pyramids, the Taj Mahal, and others. One girl told her teacher, "I don't know where to stop. I have a lot more than seven." The teacher looked at her paper and started reading her list: "To be able to see, hear, think, breathe, touch, walk, run, love, laugh …" The list went on.

We take many vital things for granted. We take for granted many of the important necessities of life we receive. Our lives are gifts from God, not our choice. So is the air, water, family, friends, church, and many things. When something we enjoy is taken away, we become upset and complain. We don't realize that it was given to us as a gift.

Manna stopped one day for the Israelites just as it had started one day. I am sure the people were upset; they had become used to falling manna every morning and had taken it for granted. They did not ask, "What did I do to deserve the best health, family or job or circumstance that I enjoy?"

I read the story about a vendor who sold bagels for fifty cents each at a street corner food stand. A jogger running past threw a couple of quarters into the bucket but didn't take a bagel. He did the same thing every day for months. One day as the jogger was passing by, the vendor stopped him. The jogger asked, "You probably want to know why I always put money in but never take a bagel, don't you?" "No," said the vendor. "I just wanted to tell you that the price of the bagel has gone up to sixty cents."

Too often, we believers treat God with that same attitude. Not only are we ungrateful for what He has given us; we also want more. Somehow, we feel God owes us good health, a comfortable life, and material blessings. Of course, God does not owe us anything, yet He gives us everything. "This is the day the Lord has made; we will rejoice and be glad in it" (Psalm 118:24). We honestly believe God owes us everything good. Sometimes, we can become so focused on one particular disappointment that we don't see the many blessings we receive every day. By being grateful for God's blessings even in the face of a disappointment, we are able to invite peace and joy into our lives and open our hearts to the many more blessings God has in store for us. We will be thankful for what we have when we remember those who are not as fortunate as we are physically, mentally or financially. We should be thankful for family members, friends, and even strangers who made it possible for us to be who we are and where we are today. We should take note of the people who are happy for our happiness and sad for our sadness and be thankful for them. We should remember those who are fighting to preserve the freedom and liberty we enjoy and be thankful.

God gave us eternal life through His Son, Jesus Christ, that we could never have earned by our works (Ephesians 2:8). No matter how hard we tried, how sincere we were, how much we gave, that would never have been enough to overcome the debt of sin. Thanksgiving opens up our hearts to know God more truly and personally. It grows our love for others and God, and it gives us the desire to be with Him. The nine lepers who did not return to Jesus to thank Him were not necessarily ungrateful people; they were most likely thankful for the healing they had received, but they just forgot about the giver. What they missed was an intimate encounter with the Lord and the chance to know Him personally.

One of the most popular Thanksgiving hymns, "Now Thank We All Our God," was written in the 1600s during the Thirty Years War in Europe. It expresses profoundly the deepest feelings of gratitude in the midst of hopelessness and destruction. Martin Rinkart and his congregation suffered when their little village in Germany was invaded. Several hundred people died, and almost everything of value was destroyed. Rinkart was brokenhearted and depressed. He spent time in prayer for days when he penned the lyrics "Now thank we all our God ... who from our mothers' arms has blessed us on our way with countless gifts of love, and still is ours today."

Thanksgiving and gratitude help us endure the hard things in life with dignity. "Give thanks in everything, for this is God's will for you in Christ Jesus" (1 Thessalonians 5:18). In every circumstance, no matter what happens or where we are, we can thank God. Not everything that happens to us is good, but God uses everything that happens to work for our good.

After receiving an abundant blessing, David brought them to the temple and prayed (1 Chronicles 29:14–16),

> But who am I, and who are my people that we should be able to give as generously as this? Everything comes from you, and we have given you only what comes from your hand. We are foreigners and strangers in your sight, as were all our ancestors. Our days on earth are like a shadow, without hope. 16 Lord our God, all this abundance that we have provided for building you a temple for your Holy Name comes

from your hand, and all of it belongs
to you.

Job was thankful for his life in this world even after he had lost everything. He said, "Naked I came from my mother's womb, and naked I will depart. The Lord gives, and the Lord takes away, blessed be the name of the Lord" (Job 1:21).

In God's plan, everything has a reason. Sometimes, we may understand it, but many times, we will not. If we want to know why the manna stopped falling, we need to know why it had started. While the Israelites were traveling in the desert, they had sheep, milk, or meat if God wanted them to eat. Manna was not a product of the earth. The people saw this on the ground and called it manna, meaning, "What is this?" (Exodus 16:15, 31).

As travelers, they could not farm or cook regularly; their focus was on reaching the Promised Land, and they needed food. In Psalm 78:24, Asaph called it "corn from heaven." It was full of nutrients and tasted like coriander seed toasted with honey (Exodus 16). It was covered with dew in the morning so the people could eat it fresh. God's provision was and is timely and at hand. The psalmist remembered this gracious gift of God when people started asking, "Can God prepare a table in the wilderness?" (Psalm 78:19). God prepared a table for them in the desert and used the dew to refrigerate it every morning (Numbers 11:7–9).

Then why did the manna stop? When Adam and Eve

sinned and were driven out of the Garden of Eden, God said that they would work with their hands and live off the earth and nature. God wanted them to live on the products of the land, the fruit of their labor. The Israelites were asked to celebrate Passover only after they reached the Promised Land, where they made bread with the produce of the land. We cannot celebrate Passover with manna (Deuteronomy 8:18). They celebrated their first Passover at Gilgal, where they made bread with the produce of the land. That's where manna stopped.

The celebration of Passover is not remembering a shameful past; it is a celebration of the Promised Land where people started eating from the work of their hands. God wants us to grow up and become self-dependent for sustenance. God does not want us to be manna people all the time. Instead of giving them handouts forever, God blessed the Israelites with skills and opportunities so they could work to earn their living. God's manna has a time and a place; we are blessed with manna at certain times as needed, and God gives us opportunities to work when the time comes. We need fulfilment, not just food. God gives us liberty to choose our paths and enjoy the fruits of our labor. He doesn't want us to be complacent and controlled by manna habits.

The manna needed to be stopped so the people could recognize their need for the living manna. God promised a land that flowed with milk and honey. The end of manna showed the faithfulness of God, who fulfills His promises.

God has a better plan for His people to enjoy the living manna and live eternally. Jesus said,

> Your fathers ate manna but they all died. But here is the bread that comes down from heaven, which anyone may eat and not die. I am the living bread that came down from heaven. Whoever eats this bread will live forever. This bread is my flesh, which I will give for the life of the world. (John 6:50)

God has given us the gift of eternal life through Jesus Christ, the living manna that came down from heaven. Grace and truth came in Jesus Christ (John 1:17). Grace is plentiful and free now. God's grace will end one day just as manna ended one day. Manna and grace are God's gracious provision; they are undeserved, and they will stop one day. They can be truly received only by a response of faith manifested in obedience. There is a difference between a symbol—manna—and reality—Christ. Manna gives only temporal life; those who ate it eventually died. But those who eat of Christ will never die. God's resources are plentiful, but they might come from the least-expected source.

Jody, a church member, said this in her testimony about her lawnmower faith.

> When I was a 5th grader I saw my father struggling in heat mowing grass. The lawn mower was too heavy for my slender dad to push. I wanted to buy a riding mower badly and started praying.

> One day I said, "Daddy I am going to buy you a riding mower." She began looking for jobs from door to door. She did several odd jobs to earn and finally saved $50. She knew it wasn't enough. Then a neighbor had a garage sale and she saw a riding lawnmower for sale. She went and told the neighbor that she badly wanted to buy her dad a riding lawn mower and asked for the price. The owner said $250. With a sad face, I was about to walk away. Then the owner asked, "How much do you have?" She said "Fifty dollars." He sold it to her for $50.

Jody believes it was God who enabled her to get the lawn mower, when she decided to step out in faith. "God is able to do immeasurably more than all we ask or imagine" (Ephesians 3:19).

All heroes of faith had to go through the manna experience. It will come at the right moment and stop at the right moment. Elijah was fed by a raven, but at God's time, the raven stopped coming and the brook dried up (1 Kings 17). God had a better and bigger plan for him.

Jonah was tired and frustrated while lying in the desert. God gave him a tree to give him shade, but in due time, a worm was sent to chew it, and the tree died (Jonah 4).

Job said, "The Lord gives, and the takes away, blessed be the name of the Lord" (Job 1:21). "Naked I came from my mother's womb, and naked I will depart."

Most Christians in South India are familiar with

Kochukunju Upadeshi, an evangelist of the nineteenth century. He toiled day and night preaching the gospel in the rural areas of Kerala, a southern state of India, often walking ten to twenty miles to do so. Often, he didn't have enough food for his family. One day he came back from a meeting and saw that his wife and son had left for her dad's home because there was nothing to eat. He felt disappointed and frustrated and fell on his knees in prayer; that was when God gave the famous Malayalam hymn, "Ente Daivam Mahathvathil Ardravanay Jeevikumbol (My God in Glory lives in Mercy)." In it, he described the abundant provision of God even in the experience of Patmos, where John the disciple spent his last days in exile. He described that God becomes the father to the orphan and a good husband to the widow, and "He can provide for me even when everyone leaves me."

# CHAPTER 7

# Made for the Mountains

Mountains are challenges on journeys whether we are walking, driving, or even flying. They can obscure our view of our path and even our destination. Some time ago, an article meant for people wanting to climb Mount Everest and other mountains in Nepal read, "The government of Nepal charges admission to climb Mount Everest. You must buy a ticket for $630 before you will be permitted to climb the 29,028-foot Mount Everest." But another sign read, "Cut-rate tickets are offered for lower peaks."

Mountain climbers are not thrilled to settle for lower peaks. When we choose to go for just the lower peaks, we miss out on the best experience on the peak that is in store for us. Climbing mountains can make us weary, impatient, and flat-out tired.

In this journey of life, there are no cut-rate deals. We tend to look for good deals, but nothing seems to get better. When we settle for lower peaks, we miss out on the bigger views on the higher ones. Climbing mountains changes our perspective. The prophet sang a song when faced with a high mountain: "The Lord God is my strength, He makes my feet like the feet of a deer; he causes me to stand on the heights" (Habakkuk 3:19).

Instead of complaining and asking God to find us another route, we should trust Him to help us climb higher. The feet of deer are made for climbing mountains. David sang the same tune: "He makes my feet like hinds' feet, and sets me upon my high places" (Psalm 18:33; 2 Samuel 22:34). We may be faced with mountains of fear, negativism, lack of self-confidence, worries, and many other negative forces that are real heights and difficult to climb over. But with faith in God, they make us stronger after we climb over them. We will mature into people of stronger faith, vision, and commitment.

Mountains can be challenging, but the Bible describes several instances when people were called to a greater purpose on mountains. Mount Ararat is considered the resting place of Noah's ark; it was where God made a covenant that He would never again destroy the world with water (Genesis 8). Noah and family witnessed the rainbow of the covenant while they were on top of the mountain.

Abraham was tested on Mount Moriah; God told him to

sacrifice Isaac there. Once Abraham acted in faith to show he was willing to offer his only son to the Lord, God stopped him and provided a ram instead as an offering. "Abraham called the name of that place, 'The Lord will provide'; as it is said to this day, 'On the mount of the Lord it shall be provided'" (Genesis 22:14).

Later in Israel's history, King David selected this location as a site to build a temple for the Lord (2 Samuel 24:18). He did not build the temple, but he did make preparations for his son, Solomon, to do so. That temple served as the central place for Jewish worship for approximately 400 years until its destruction by the Babylonians under King Nebuchadnezzar in 587–586 BC.

Moses saw the burning bush while he was tending sheep on Mount Horeb (Exodus 3). This is the same mountain later on called Mount Sinai, which God asked Moses to climb to receive the Ten Commandments (Exodus 33).

There are many other important mountains such as Mount Carmel, where Elijah saw the glory of God. Peter, James, and John were tired just as were the other disciples when Jesus asked them to go up the mountain where He was transfigured (Matthew 17; Mark 9; Luke 9). They saw God's glory shining on Jesus's face, something they had not seen or imagined before that. They saw Moses and Elijah coming to witness the anointing of the Son of God. A bright cloud covered them, and a voice from the cloud said, "This is my Son, whom I love; with him I am well pleased. Listen to him!" When the disciples heard this, they fell facedown to the ground, terrified. The other disciples missed the experience. Christians are made for mountain climbing. We are created to climb higher in our faith, love, and hope.

Nature students say that when hawks are attacked by crows or other birds, they don't resist; rather, they fly higher and in wider circles. The attacking birds will no longer feel safe following the hawk, and they give up and descend. As people of faith, we need to rise higher above the forces of evil that show up in the form of discrimination based on color, gender, class, race, and other forms of injustice. Every day, that invitation calls us to abandon old perspectives and take up a new vision that proclaims the love of God. Our purpose is to live on a plane that is higher than the world's plane.

A mountain guide was taking a group of tourists on a hike along a mountain trail. As they were climbing, they came to a particularly treacherous place on the trail. A high, rocky, steep side was on the left, and a deep drop-off was on the right. The path was only two feet wide in places. The guide warned the tourists, "Be very careful along here. It's a very dangerous part of the trail. But if you fall, remember to look to the right. At least you'll get a wonderful view on the way down."

We might not be able to rise above our life situations due to temptations and influences. We may be tempted to act like the rest of the world because goodness and moral virtues are considered weaknesses in many places. In such situations, even if we don't feel like succeeding, we can hope to do our best in the situation and know that one day, good will triumph over evil. Just as the face of Moses shone while he was on the top of Mount Sinai (Exodus 34:29), our faces will shine like stars in this dark world. Paul said, "And we all, who with unveiled faces contemplate the Lord's glory, are being transformed into his image with ever-increasing glory, which comes from the Lord, who is the Spirit" (2 Corinthians 3:18).

When we face mountains in our lives, we should not be afraid because God has a higher plain for us to experience. We are not to settle for less just because achieving lower heights seems to be easier. We should learn to fly higher when trials and temptations come. Johnson Oatman, who wrote "Count Your Blessing," wrote the famous hymn "Higher Ground," which was based on Philippians 3:14: "I press on towards the goal to win the prize for which God has called me heavenward in Christ Jesus."

> I'm pressing on the upward way,
> New heights I'm gaining every day;
> My heart has no desire to stay
> Where doubts arise and fears dismay;
> Though some may dwell where those abound,
> My prayer, my aim, is higher ground.
> I want to scale the utmost height
> And catch a gleam of glory bright;
> But still I'll pray till Heav'n I've found,
> Lord, plant my feet on higher ground.

A mountain guide in Switzerland taught people how to climb. He climbed many of the highest peaks in the country. The villagers all knew him and loved him. One day, the news came that while climbing a difficult cliff, he had slipped and fallen to his death. They commissioned a sculptor to carve a statue of him they wanted to set up at the exact location where he fell. The sculptor carved him in his alpine hat and cleated shoes with his rope and axe. The statue was shaped showing him the very act of climbing. To eulogize their friend, the community added these words to the base of the sculpture: "He died climbing."

We are made for the mountains; they were made for us to climb. Like the deer, we have feet given by the Creator to climb to higher planes. We should be found climbing higher and higher every day in our life journeys and hope that one day it will be said of us, "He died climbing."

## CHAPTER 8

# Living with Lions

Many times, we wonder why bad things happen to good people. Our journeys can become suddenly rough and fierce. We will be tried for no reason of our own making. The world is a fallen place in which we strive to live righteous lives.

In Romans 8:22, Paul said that creation, which had been damaged and broken by sin, was groaning for redemption. We groan as we wait for the redemption of our bodies. We live with scars of sin in and around us. We have to face injustice. The widow of one of the people who perished in the 9/11 plane crash in Pennsylvania wrote the book *Let's Roll*. She wrote,

Many miracles, however, are not
a change to the normal course of
human events; they're found in God's
ability and desire to sustain and
nurture people through even the worst
situations. Somewhere along the way,
I stopped demanding that God fix the
problems in my life and started to be
thankful for his presence as I endured
them.

Daniel was a good man who led a life faithful to God. He was always honest and did things in a way that pleased God and others. King Darius was so pleased with him that he made Daniel the next most important person in his huge kingdom; everything Daniel said became the law of the land.

However, a time came when some other people in charge who weren't quite as important as Daniel became jealous of him, and they set out to find fault with him. They knew the only fault they could find to tell the king about him was that Daniel always worshipped his God. So they went to the king with a scheme; they made out that they wanted to honor the king, and they asked him to decree that for thirty days, no one could worship anyone besides the king under penalty of death.

Of course the king thought that it would be great if everyone worshipped him, so he signed the law. They carefully watched Daniel praying to God three times a day as he always did, and they reported that to the king. King Darius tried everything he could think of to save Daniel from his punishment, but sadly, he had to agree to the punishment, and that evening, Daniel was thrown into the den of starving lions.

The book of Daniel stands out as a great example of how to live in the midst of fire, lions, and death sentences. Chapter 1 shows how the young men refused to eat Babylonian food, which would have defiled them. In chapter 2, Daniel interpreted Nebuchadnezzar's dream. In chapter 3, we see a friend in the fiery furnace. In chapter 4, we learn that Nebuchadnezzar lost his kingdom and was exiled to the forest and lived like an animal. In chapter 5, we see King Belshazzar start and end his reign. And in chapter 6, we see a Persian king, Darius.

Daniel had served under at least three kings by that time. About sixty years had passed since the events in chapter 3—the fiery furnace. Belshazzar became king, who some historians say was Nebuchadnezzar's grandson. And after that, Darius took over the kingdom. As one historian put it, "The sunset of Babylon's kingdom has now become the dawning of the Medo-Persian Empire."

According to scholars, the Darius in chapter 6 refers to Cyrus the Great, the Persian ruler who eventually allowed the Jews to return to Jerusalem seventy years after they had been taken into captivity. Daniel was no longer a young man then; he was perhaps eighty; everything was going well for Daniel, who had been made the chief of the governors. But then according to the new decree, he would have to face the lions. He went up to the upper room and prayed three times as he used to do.

When we find out about decrees written against us—layoff notices, bounced checks, foreclosures, collections, bad medical diagnoses, news of a loved one's death—we should go to our upper rooms, to a higher level. We are to rise above our problems rather than be distracted by them, get on our knees, and pour out to God. Prayer can change negative judgments, decrees, and diagnoses.

The lions Daniel would have to face were violent and fierce, but the other lions, those who plotted against him, schemed and planned behind the scenes while looking nice and good. The king had not intended to harm Daniel, but those other lions had tricked him.

Do you realize you are being watched? Now more than ever, all of us are being watched and more than we realize. Security cameras are tracking us everywhere—in stores and on the road. Credit card companies are watching what we buy. Phone companies are watching whom we call and who is calling us. And we will never know how closely we are being watched as we surf the internet.

They watched Daniel and saw him praying as he had for decades. That could have been his last prayer. The world around is deceitful. Verse 5 of chapter 6 reads, "We will never find any basis for charges against this man Daniel unless it has something to do with the law of his God." Daniel was being watched by the lions that were looking to harm him.

King Darius was so worried about Daniel that he would not have anything to eat and he couldn't sleep all night. But Daniel probably had sound sleep because the lions were so quiet.

At dawn, Darius hurried to the den and called out, "Daniel, God's servant! Has your God been able to save you from the lions?" He must have been very surprised to hear Daniel say, "Yes, King Darius, my God sent His angel to shut the lions' mouths, and they haven't even touched me. That's because I never did any wrong to God, and I haven't done any wrong to you either." King Darius was delighted to hear Daniel and ordered the guards to pull him out of the den and its hungry and ferocious lions.

We may have to live with lions at times. Pain and suffering, disappointments and failures are among the lions that can take away our peace, but God will protect us from them.

Years ago, I had severe shoulder pain that required a long time of physical therapy. It was so bad that I could not put on my shirt without someone's help. During that time, I worked and went to physical therapy every other day for about six months. I used to say that those physical therapy rooms were torture chambers. The therapist would talk to me so nicely in the beginning and engage in some interesting conversation and then quickly pull my arm back swiftly. It was so painful that I had to take pain medication before going to the therapist. I asked my wife to go with me several times so she could watch the doctor and stop him from hurting me. During those times, I felt a lion was frightening me. But God's grace healed me, and I now can raise my hands high to praise Him.

When Jim, a member of our church, was in the hospital awaiting open-heart surgery, he received the shocking news that his only son had been instantly killed in an accident. Jim was inconsolable. "Why not me instead of him?" he cried out to God. When it seemed he had no more tears to shed, a gentle calm came over him. "It was as if the Holy Spirit surrounded me," Jim explained, "and my troubled spirit finally rested. I still didn't understand why, but I did have the assurance that my boy was safe with my heavenly Father and experienced a peace that only God could bring."

Not long before his death, Jesus told His disciples that a time would come when their faith would be tested to the point of abandoning Him. But He also assured them that they would find peace, be united by a strengthened faith, and ultimately share in His victory. That seems to be the journey often experienced by Christ's followers when trouble strikes—first shock and despair, but after a while comes the calming sense of the Holy Spirit's presence and the comforting awareness, "We are not alone!" A welcome peace eventually comes—just as Jesus promised. But no matter what our circumstances are, God is still with us, and we will share in His ultimate victory.

Many of you may be in situations like that, looking at the

schedules of chemo or radiation, surgery or therapy. Some of you may have infirmities that limit your mobility. Some of you may have disabilities or conditions that you have to carry with you all your life. Whatever lion is looking hungrily at you, in the midst of that is a peace God will bring if you look up to Him.

There are fierce lions we have to live with at certain times. Paul had a thorn in the flesh that he had to live with that he described in 2 Corinthians 12.

> Three times I pleaded with the Lord to take it away from me. But he said to me, "My grace is sufficient for you, for my power is made perfect in weakness." Therefore I will boast all the more gladly about my weaknesses, so that Christ's power may rest on me.

Peace is not the absence of troubles; it is the presence of God in the middle of trouble. A major art gallery sponsored a competition for painters; they offered a prize for the best painting on the subject of peace. The painting that won was a real surprise. The scene was the ocean in a violent storm. The sky was ominous with lightning cutting across the sky and waves crashing into the rock walls of the cliffs by the shore. There, about halfway up the cliff, was a bird nest tucked into a tiny hollow in the rock. A mother bird was sitting on that nest with her little babies tucked underneath her sleeping soundly. Peace is not just the absence of a storm; it is rest in the middle of a storm. Many of us could use that kind of peace right now, and it is the kind of peace we can have right now while living with lions.

Psalm 46 describes the incredible peace God offers: "God is our refuge and strength, an ever-present help in trouble." The more troubled things are, the more present God makes Himself. The psalmist said, "Therefore we will not fear, though the earth give way and the mountains fall into the heart of the sea, though its waters roar and foam and the mountains quake with their surging." Everything's collapsing, even things that have always been good and strong for us. Have no fear because "God is our refuge and strength."

Verse 4 of the psalm reads, "There is a river whose streams make glad the city of God, the holy place where the Most High dwells." God lives today in those who belong to Him through faith in Jesus. "God is within her, and she will not fall … Nations are in uproar, kingdoms fall … the Lord Almighty is with us; the God of Jacob is our fortress" (vv. 5–7). Then, as everything seems to be melting down, God says, "Be still, and know that I am God" (Psalm 46:10).

Rake Sueh was in Chinese prison for eight years for a crime he did not commit. His family rejected him in the fear of the harassment from police and the government. He wrote,

> That meant I had lost my son forever.
> This drove me into an abyss of
> despair. Thoughts of suicide lingered

in my mind continually. I lived in both physical and emotional darkness. After trying to pray, that night I dreamed that an unidentified light healed the wounds of my heart. Today I know that light was Jesus Christ. From the time of that experience to today, I faithfully pray. Also, I joined a secret Bible study that meets twice a week. Gradually the wounds in my heart have begun to heal. I have come to understand what it means to have peace in a prison. God will accompany us when we are walking through our darkest times. (See Ps. 23:4.) I had a great surprise when we celebrated the Chinese New Year in prison! My ex-wife and my son whom I had not seen for five years came to pay me a visit. Now I know what amazing grace is.

Shirley Ceasar has sung a beautiful song, "Peace in the Midst of the Storm."

> Now when my spirit has been broken
> Till it's masked by misery
> When the doctor shakes his head and look forlorn
> Jesus comes to make my bedside
> A cathedral of faith and love
> He'll give you peace in the midst of the storm.

Jesus said, "I have told you these things, so that in me you may have peace. In this world you will have trouble, but take heart! I have overcome the world" (John 16:33). Through the cross, we can overcome "because the one who is in you is greater than the one who is in the world" (1 John 4:4). Only in Christ can we have peace in the lions' den. Many times, we don't know the real lions. Daniel was not in the lions' den; rather, the poor lions were in Daniel's den. They were so afraid that they couldn't do a thing, and they couldn't wait for Daniel to get out. John Wesley said, "If we fear God and nothing else, we will win. If we fear everything else and don't fear God, we will be defeated." When we fear God, we will not be afraid of anything else.

# CHAPTER 9

# Honey in the Lion

The story of Samson in the book of Judges is a strange story of a warrior eating honey from the remains of a lion. Samson is a unique and strange character in the Bible. He was from a Jewish family chosen by God to lead Israel to fight against their chief enemy, the Philistines.

Samson was born by a special birth as we read in Judges 13:2. An angel of God visited his parents and gave his mother a revelation. She did not have a child for a long time. The angel told her that she would have a son and that she should follow certain rules before his birth. The newborn should not cut his hair forever because his hair would be the source of his strength.

Indeed, he became a very strong man. Samson was like

Hercules or Superman, a man of superhuman strength (Judges 14). God gave him immense strength. He killed a thousand Philistines with the jawbone of a donkey. At times, he was a madman. He tied up three hundred foxes tail to tail and set them on fire; they raced off and burned the enemy's wheat fields. He murdered thirty men for their clothes. Philistines were very afraid of him. But he sadly fell for an enemy woman's seduction; his hair was cut (Judges 16), and he lost his superhuman strength. He had a weakness for women, which is a story in itself. But there is something good we can learn from Samson's life about how we can overcome challenges and use them as a source of strength for the future.

Samson loved riddles with surprising solutions. Choosing the appropriate answer is the key to a riddle. Young children love to ask and be asked riddles. What follows you wherever you go, and you leave more of them behind you the farther you go? Footsteps. What comes once a year, twice a week, but never in a day? The letter *E*. Riddles are fun, but some can offer insights into life.

One of Samson's meaningful riddles was, "Out of the eater came something to eat" (Judges 14:14). It teaches the meaning of how tough people deal with tough circumstances. Tough times will not last long, but tough people do. Samson was a tough man. When it was time for him to get a wife, he went on his own to a distant country against his parents' wishes and away from his own people; he traveled through a rugged land. On the way, he tore apart a fierce lion with his bare hands.

Sometime later, he was traveling the same road and decided to take a look at his old victim. He came across the carcass of the lion. A swarm of bees had taken up home inside the dry hide and remains. He scooped out honey and went on his happy journey. He ate some and gave some to his parents and friends, but he didn't tell them the source. He coined this riddle for them to figure out: "Out of the eater came something to eat."

Rev. J. Ellsworth Kalas wrote a beautiful piece about Samson: "Blessed are those who learn that there is honey in the lion." Some lions in the journey of life are not wild beasts like the one Samson met, but some can be worse, and we might not be able to run from them or kill them. Samson's outlook on facing lions in life was unique and bold; he found nourishment in the lion that had threatened his life.

We face social and political lions in our world—violence, poverty, racism, injustice, discrimination, exploitation, and greed are among them. Nations fight each other to establish control and power over each other. They can maim us for life. None of us likes these lions, but we can see honey that can come out of these lions. Nothing good can possibly come out of a world war, but honey came out of World War II. Scientists agree that we made greater progress in the development of medicine during those years than we would have in a whole generation of peace, and this is especially true in the development of antibiotics. Some may argue we could have possibly achieved that without the war, but the war made it essential and quicker. If we look for honey, we can find it in even the worst situations. We can find honey in lions.

Churches are not immune to the presence of lions. Any active church will face critical issues and serious attacks from lions. Lions intimidate and terrorize more than anything. Some will see a split coming, and others will say the church will die, and others can become paralyzed by the fear they provoke. When we are faced with lions, we should not be intimidated or threatened; rather, we must be empowered and emboldened by God's power and grace to tackle these problems. That is what the power of the Spirit given to Samson did. It is the same Spirit given to us.

Girl Scouts receive a little survival guide book during their training that teaches them how to survive in the woods or at sea if they are alone. The book describes how to respond to a mountain lion—by running, climbing a tree, singing a song, or standing still covering your head with your jacket? The correct answer is the last one. By covering your head, you can make yourself look bigger than your enemy.

In our journey of faith, we need to remember that God is greater than our greatest problem. If we fail once, we should not be afraid; God will help us get up and try again. As believers of Jesus Christ, we are overcomers; in 1 John

5:4–5, we read, "For everyone born of God overcomes the world. This is the victory that has overcome the world, even our faith. Who is it that overcomes the world? Only the one who believes that Jesus is the Son of God."

Only a courageous person would go back to a place where he or she was attacked by a lion, but Samson was courageous as well as curious. We often hear, "We've tried that before, we've gone that way before, so there's no point in trying again." But we are Christians; we are overcomers, and everyone born of God overcomes the world. This is the victory that has overcome the world.

A story in the news was about a driving instructor in Germany who had been teaching others how to drive and obtain licenses for forty-six years though he never had a driver's license. The first time he tried to get one, he failed the test, and he never again had the confidence that he could pass the test. Failure isn't defeat until we stop trying. God gives us opportunities over and over, and it's up to us to overcome the fear and try again.

Many lions attack the faith in the form of rules and government policies. It is very difficult in some Muslim countries and under Communist regimes to openly worship God. Consider the courageous midwives Shirpa and Puah, who had been ordered by Pharaoh to kill all the Hebrew baby boys (Exodus 1:15–21). But these brave women feared God more than they feared Pharaoh and did not do what he had told them to do; they let the boys live. God vindicated their stand: "God was kind to them and gave them families of their own."

In the Book of Acts chapter 4, we read that when the Jewish leaders instructed Peter and John not to speak or teach at all in the name of Jesus, they replied, "Judge for yourselves whether it is right in God's sight to obey you rather than God" (Acts 4:18–19). Jesus said,

> I tell you friends, do not be afraid of those who kill the body and after that can do no more. But I will show you whom you should fear. Fear him who, after the killing of the body, has power to throw you into hell. Yes, I tell you fear him. (Luke 12:4–5)

John Wesley, the founder of Methodism, said, "Give me a dozen people who hate nothing but sin and fear no one but God and we can turn England upside down." Wesley himself, beaten up more than once, feared no human being; neither magistrate nor bishop nor thug. "Hate only sin," he said, "fear only God, and you will then fear nothing else."

We face a lot of lions in our personal lives. Some of them are visible, but many are very subtle. We have job situations, personal relationship issues, sickness, bereavement, disappointments, and disillusionment that can be fierce. Some simply give up and throw pity parties, and others become bitter and revengeful and take the attitude, "Get others before they get you." This kind of negativity has made the world an evil place full of hatred and violence.

Others like Samson simply find a riddle in it and discover a secret—the honey in it, the good that can come from a bad situation. We need to contend for that honey we get from our lions because it tastes the sweetest. John Milton wrote his greatest works *Paradise Lost* and *Paradise Regained* in the darkness of his blindness. John Bunyan wrote *Pilgrim's Progress* in the dark corner of a prison cell, and Beethoven was partially deaf when he composed many of his great musical works. Our sweetest songs are those that tell of our saddest thoughts.

When I look back at the difficulties I have been through—the pains of sickness and the brokenness of sadness—the honey God provided me was the sweetest I had ever tasted. Sometimes, we may have to pass our way of lions again, but that can become a source of strength. After a second or third recurrence of a disease, a grief, or a broken relationship, we can say, "Oh yes—I've passed this place before and might do so again." Or we can be a source of comfort to someone who is passing through that place now.

In 2 Corinthians 12:7–9, Paul wrote,

> I was given a thorn in my flesh, I prayed three times to take it away, and God said to me, "My grace is sufficient for you, for my power is made perfect in weakness." Therefore I will boast all the more gladly about my weaknesses, so that Christ's power may rest on me. That is why, for Christ's sake, I delight

in weaknesses, for when I am weak,
and then I am strong.

In Romans 8, Paul exhorted us to be more than conquerors through Jesus Christ, who loved us. Nothing in this world—tribulation, distress, persecution, famine, nakedness, peril, or sword—can separate us from our loving God. In all these things, we are more than conquerors through He who loves us. He wrote,

> For I am convinced that neither death
> nor life, neither angels nor demons,
> neither the present nor the future, nor
> any powers, neither height nor depth,
> nor anything else in all creation, will
> be able to separate us from the love of
> God that is in Christ Jesus our Lord.

Many of us may be facing visible or not-so visible lions—sickness, old age, job loss, family problems, work issues, financial troubles, and many other lions. Then there are the invisible ones like addictions, jealousy, pride, and doubt. The story of the heroes of faith such as Daniel and Samson teach us that we are not trapped by any lions. Like Samson, Paul, Daniel, and many others, we can find honey in the lions, power in weakness, and sweetness in tragedy, and success in failure if we look for it. God is on our side, and victory is ours. That is the faith that overcomes.

Roger lost his job due to the company being downsized. For months, he searched, applied for jobs, prayed, asked others to pray, and trusted God. Roger and his wife, Jerrie, prayed for several months, and their emotions fluctuated. They saw God provide for them in unexpected ways and experienced His grace, but sometimes, they worried that a job would never come. For fifteen long months, they waited.

Then Roger had three interviews with a company, and a week later, the employment agency called and said, "Have you heard the saying that sometimes clouds have a silver lining? Well, you got the job!"

Jerrie wrote in her blog: "We wouldn't trade this hard experience for anything else. It brought us closer together and closer to the Lord. Friends who had prayed rejoiced and gave thanks to God. The writer of Hebrews reminds us, 'Let us hold fast the confession of our hope without wavering, for He who promised is faithful'" (Hebrews 10:23).

Mark Twain was the great American writer, humorist, entrepreneur, publisher, and lecturer. Among his novels are *The Adventures of Tom Sawyer* and its sequel, *The Adventures of Huckleberry Finn*, the latter often called the great American novel.

At one point in his life, Twain was so poor that he lost his house and property. A newspaper took up a collection to help him, but he declined the money saying that he had decided not to accept anything free from anyone. Seven months later, he finished *The Adventures of Tom Sawyer*, which became a success and made him more money than anyone can imagine.

We will find something to eat in the eater only if we look

for it. We are faced with fierce problems such as war, famine, and natural disasters that are beyond our control, but we can seek the honey in them. These things bring nothing good if we look at them casually.

My wife and I faced difficulties in the early days of our family raising two children; we both worked and went to school. But we thank God for that, and we treasure those hard times. It is through those experiences that we learned to trust in God and that our children became rooted in the faith in a faithful God. Thank God for sickness. During that time, one of our children would often become very sick due to allergies and asthma. We struggled in faith when we prayed. But because of his sickness, he decided to become a source of help to other children. Years later, we look back and thank God because we now can identify with the comfort he brings as a pediatrician to other young couples with children.

The psalmist who wrote Psalm 119 thanked God for affliction in verse 71: "It was good for me to be afflicted." The lions in our journeys will make us stronger. Like Samson, we may pass them again one day and draw strength from them for the rest of our journeys, allowing us to become sources of help for others. God comforts us not just so we will be comfortable but also so we will be sources of comfort for others. That's the answer to life's riddle.

# CHAPTER 10

# Decisions Determine Destiny

Our choices are very important no matter how small or big they seem. Each decision follows an action that will stay with us. A presidential candidate was asked why he had not enlisted when the Vietnam War was going on. He could have answered that he had the legal right to do so, but instead, he candidly replied, "I didn't know back then that I'd be standing before you today." Many others have said, "If only I had known, I would have done things differently than I did."

People find it hard to make important decisions. They try to avoid them or try to find someone else to make decisions for them. "If you do not choose your way, you may end up where you are heading," said Buddha. Many people put off decisions about eternity and salvation as long as possible. But like it or not, their decisions will decide their destinies. Good intentions are not enough. They know that they are important, but they don't want to make decisions.

In the gospel according to Matthew (chapter 25), Jesus taught by a parable of ten women who were waiting for the groom. Five of them did not take enough oil, and their lamps were running out of it. While they were away buying more oil, the bridegroom came, and thus they lost their opportunity to meet him. The other five who had oil in reserve were able to join the groom for the wedding feast. Timely decisions are more important than good intentions. There are no unbelievers in hell, just believers who waited too long to believe. I have heard many regretting that they had not stopped their smoking, drinking or drug habits earlier. To have a destiny requires choosing one at the right time. Every action has a reaction.

"Control your own destiny or someone else will," Jack Welch, former CEO of GE, said. Ronald Reagan learned at an early age that it was better to make a decision than to let others make it for you. When he was a kid, his aunt took him to a shoe store and had the shoemaker make him a pair of shoes. He was asked if he wanted square or round toes, but he couldn't make up his mind. When he went to pick them up, he saw that one shoe was round-toed and the other was square-toed. The shoemaker was trying to teach him a lesson. If you don't make decisions in a timely manner, someone else might and you might not like it.

God owns our lives, but we choose our destinies. God gave us the freedom to choose but not the freedom not to choose. To decide not to choose good is always a choice to choose evil. Jesus said, "He that is not with Me is against Me" (Matthew 12:30). In other words, if you do not use your freedom to choose good, you are choosing to be with evil.

You are not free to choose the consequences of your choices. God has given us full control of our choices. Our responses and decisions do matter. Decisions determine destiny. "The only person you are destined to become is the person you decide to be," Ralph Waldo Emerson wrote. Jesus said to Peter, "Whatever you bind on earth will be bound in heaven" (Matthew 16:18). Whatever we do here will have an impact on our destinies. We can serve the world consciously and unconsciously, but we can serve God only consciously. The priorities we set are clear indications of where we are heading and whom we are serving whether we admit it or not. When it comes down to serving God, it's a choice we have to make voluntarily. "I have set before you life and death, blessings and curses" (Deuteronomy 30:19).

Our choices will affect not only our lives but also those of others around us and those who come after us. We are all living in a world of past decisions. Our lives here and now were affected by our decisions. Our taxes, health care, and moral and social values are products of decisions made by others in the past. We need to make good and conscious decisions for others to follow us in the journey.

Once I read about a certain court building that stands in a unique location in a city in the United States. Raindrops that fall on the north side of the building go into Lake Ontario and the Gulf of St. Lawrence, while those falling on the south side go into the Mississippi River and the Gulf of Mexico. At precisely the point of the peak of the roof, just a gentle puff of wind can determine the destiny of many raindrops. It will make a difference of over two thousand miles as to their final destination. Our decisions decide where we will spend eternity.

There are only two eternal destinies. Jesus talked about the narrow way and the broad way (Matthew 7), no third way. These two ways never merge, and we cannot choose both. "No one can serve two masters; for either he will hate the one and love the other, or else he will be loyal to the one and despise the other. You cannot serve God and mammon" (Matthew 6:24).

Jesus taught a parable about a rich man and the poor Lazarus (Luke 16). The rich man lived a life of extreme luxury. At the steps of his house lived Lazarus, a poor man. The rich man was completely indifferent to the plight of Lazarus; he showed him no love, sympathy, or compassion. When they died, Lazarus went to heaven, and the rich man went to hell. In the parable, the rich man was not guilty of any gross sin, but he had lived a life with no view to eternity. His problem was not being rich. Being wealthy is not evil. Abraham for instance was a wealthy man. But the rich man in the parable failed to lay up treasures in heaven though the opportunity to do so literally lay at his doorstep every day.

At the Billy Graham crusade in Seattle in 1994, a woman named Shirley Lansing gave a testimony that was deeply moving. She told the crowd, "I come with a story about my son, John Kendall Morgan. He was a warrant officer in the United States Army, serving in Operation Desert Storm." She told the crowd that her son had committed his life to Jesus at an early age.

> At that time, it didn't seem terribly important, but it was ... A few weeks ago, two officers came to our door and told us they regretted to inform us that our son had been killed in action. His helicopter had been shot down by hostile Iraqi fire ... When Jack got on the airplane to leave for Saudi Arabia, he gave Lisa, his fiancée, a bride's book. They were planning their wedding ... I speak to you only from my heart, and out of my pain, because only God can give me the strength to stand here before you and say these words. But they're so important. Each of you has the decision to make that my son made. And this is the time when you have a choice, because we never know how long we'll have to make that decision.

Three weeks before John Morgan was killed in action half a world from home, he wrote two letters to his family "just in case." Shirley and her family gathered to read the letters after they received word that he had died. John's words reassured his family; his letter ended, "In case you have to open this, please don't worry. I am all right. Now I know something you don't know—what heaven's like!"

CHAPTER 11

# Clouds

C loudy skies are not looked upon as pleasant days for a journey. We often wish for blue skies instead of storm clouds. But many times, cloudy skies reveal God's faithfulness. We gain perspective on how God has been faithful in our trials as we look back on the clouds. The psalmist looked at the clouds and wrote, "God makes the clouds his chariot" (Psalm 104:3).

We live in the age of "cloud services." Recently, I was looking for some pictures that I took on my phone but could not find. When I searched for them in different ways, it said that my pictures were backed up in the cloud. Companies like Google and Amazon are competing to have everyone in the cloud. Our lives are in the cloud now. Cloud computing is based on the time-sharing model we leveraged years ago before we could afford our own computers. The idea is to share computing power among many companies and people, thereby reducing the cost of that computing power for those who leverage it. A cloud of data pervades the whole wide earth and holds all the information everyone feeds into it knowingly or unknowingly. When you search anything online, buy something with a credit card, or send back a survey, all that information becomes part of the cloud. If time and money is spent, all that information can be tracked down to some hardware hosted out of somewhere in the world.

In the early days of online services, people were more conscious about guarding their privacy. Now, with the advent of a large number of social media platforms, every person has every detail of his or her profile and history in the cloud. We cannot live without the cloud anymore.

Clouds bring perspective. In the history of the Israelites, God communicated with the people through the clouds. Someone jokingly said, "Moses was the first person with a tablet downloading data from the cloud"—the Ten Commandments.

Our perspective of the sky changes when we see clouds. When movies of air exercises and aerial combats are filmed, directors wait for some clouds to serve not only as a backdrop but also to give a sense of movement to the planes. Numbers 14:14 says that the Israelites were the witness to the world; the cloud was their GPS in that horrible wilderness.

God gave directions to the journey of the Israel in the desert through the presence of a cloud. That cloud others thought to be so unwelcome was their daily scout. When the cloud moved, they moved; when it stalled, they stood still. "But if the cloud were not taken up, then they did not journey till the day it was taken up" (Exodus 40:37). As long as the cloud abode upon the tabernacle, they rested in their tents (Numbers 9:18). There were probably times when nothing happened for two days, a week, a month, or even a year. When the cloud settled on them, they stayed. The people must have complained, "When will God ever get us going again? We have been waiting for a long time. The promise is delayed."

We may have been praying and waiting for a change in our situation for a long time. It seems like forever, and the inaction and idleness are becoming intolerable and painful. We tend to ask if God has forgotten us just as Asaph did in Psalm 77. It will take time to learn that there was a good reason God stalled the cloud. God's timing is better than ours when it comes to the journey of life. More often, when the cloud stalls, God is at work for His children. Israel's cloud stalled one day so God could set up a battle line to stop the enemy. Job prayed in despair while he was waiting for the cloud of suffering to change. He lamented, "May the day perish on which I was born ... May a cloud settle on it" (Job 3:3–5). The cloud, that misty covering that often falls on God's people, is not a blot on God's judgment or a warning of a storm; it is a place of divine communication. Clouds are instruments of divine love by which God gives direction to those who listen to Him.

The cloud has always been and always will be viewed in two ways: darkness to some and brightness to others. It depends on their perspective, how they view the cloud. To outsiders, it may look dark and gloomy and make them ask, "If their God is so powerful, why do they not have sunshine all the time? Why do they suffer daily under that gloomy cloud? Everywhere they go, the cloud appears." But to the people of God, the cloud was a divine sign for them to trust in God's guidance. To the people who were left over from the great flood of Noah, it was in the dark clouds that a rainbow appeared as the covenant of God's promise not to destroy earth by water again. God set a rainbow in the cloud as an everlasting sign of His faithfulness. "And the bow shall be in the cloud; and I will look upon it, that I may remember the everlasting covenant between God and every living creature of all flesh that is upon the earth" (Genesis 9:16). It is the signal of communication in the cloud not to be afraid no matter how dark it seems. When we look at the clouds, we can look for God, who makes His chariots in the clouds.

We think of clouds as difficulties and obstacles on our journeys, but rainy and cloudy days are realities we deal with daily. God has used clouds as a means of delivering His people. David wrote in Psalm 18,

He parted the heavens and came
down; dark clouds were under his
feet. He mounted the cherubim and
flew; He soared on the wings of the
wind. He made darkness his covering,
His canopy around Him, the dark rain
clouds of the sky. Out of the brightness
of His presence clouds advanced.

David sang this song the day God delivered him from the enemy. They turned out to be clouds of victory and deliverance for David. He didn't know until it was all over what the storm was all about. No doubt David sat trembling in a cave while the lightning and hail struck the ground and deafening thunder shook it. *What does it all mean?* David must have asked himself. *Here I am fighting a terrible enemy. Now, I have to sit here hopeless under these fearful, scary clouds.* But when the storm passed and the cloud lifted, he looked about and did not see any enemies. God had sent the clouds, thunder, and lightning to deliver him. God comes in a cloud and answers with thunder as we read, "I answered you out of a thundercloud" (Psalm 81:7).

The Israelites were surrounded by the Philistines, who wanted to attack them and take over the kingdom (1 Samuel 7). The prophet Samuel called out to the living God when the Philistines drew near to engage Israel in battle. "But that day the Lord thundered with loud thunder against the Philistines and threw them into such a panic that they were routed before the Israelites."

If we see clouds that darken the day, hear deafening thunder, and see lighting striking all around us during our journey, we can rest assured that the almighty God is working for our victory.

CHAPTER 12

# Stones in the Way

One of the places we lived is known as Grey Stone because of a nearby area with large stones. These stones have proven to be a nuisance over the years, but they have also given our structures and land great strength. During the journey of life, we all will step on and over many stones in our paths. Stones can be of different types and nature. Some of them may be big and heavy, and others may seem small and light. They could have been there by nature or placed by someone or something that had happened before.

We will come across stones of contentment and complacency in the journey. After the rule of King Solomon, Israel was divided and scattered. Around 600 BC, King Nebuchadnezzar of Babylon invaded them, and many

Israelites were taken captive to Babylon. Jerusalem was destroyed, the walls were knocked down, the temple was burned, and the city was turned into a heap of stones.

About one hundred years later, Zerubbabel, a leader of the Jews in captivity, took about fifty thousand Israelites and returned to rebuild the temple. Unfortunately, they became discouraged and quit because of the opposition from the enemies and Kings Xerxes and Artaxerxes (Ezra 4). God then sent them the prophets Haggai and Zechariah to encourage them to finish the project.

The story of Nehemiah occurred around 438 BC. Persians took over Babylon eventually. Nehemiah, a Jew was chosen by King Artaxerxes of Persia as his cupbearer, and later, he became a governor (Nehemiah 1:11). Though he was in a foreign land, his life was going well; he had position and power. He heard that the wall of Jerusalem was broken down, its gates had been burned, and the city was just a heap of rubble. He wept, fasted, and prayed, and then he decided to do something about it.

When we receive troubling news, we naturally weep about it, but we have to get beyond that and do something about it. Many times, we are either content with the way things are or quit trying because of past failures. There have been leaders like Zerubbabel who could not complete the work. We may feel inadequate when compared to those leaders who failed.

Bette Nesmith had a good secretarial job in a Dallas bank when she ran across a problem that interested her.

She explored and found a better way to make corrections to letters typed on an electric typewriter. Bette had some art experience and she knew that artists who worked in oils just painted over their error. Maybe that would work for her too. So she concocted a fluid to paint cover her typing errors. Before long, all the secretaries in her building were using what she then called 'MistakeOut' She attempted to sell the product idea to marketing agencies and various companies (including IBM), but they turned her down. However, secretaries continued to like her product, so Bette Nesmith used her kitchen as her first manufacturing facility and she started selling it on her own. When Bette Nesmith sold the enterprise, the tiny white bottles were earning $3.5 million in profits annually on sales of $38 million. The buyer was Gillette Company and the sale price was $47.5 million. That was one obstacle Bette Nesmith was glad she had to face.

Nehemiah gathered his leaders and said, "Come, let us rebuild Jerusalem, and we will no longer be in disgrace." Nehemiah led a small group to Jerusalem. He found that the stones were not the only problems they faced. They had to face the stones of heavy ridicule and condemnation. In Nehemiah 2, we read that when Sanballat the Horonite, Tobiah the Ammonite official, and Geshem the Arab heard about it, they mocked and ridiculed them. Nehemiah told them, "The God of heaven will give us success. We his servants will start rebuilding, but as for you, you have no share in Jerusalem." In Nehemiah 4:2, we read that they said,

What are those feeble Jews doing?
Will they restore their wall? Will they
finish in a day? Can they bring the
stones back to life from those heaps
of rubble—burned as they are? Even a
fox climbing up on it would break down
their wall of stones.

The ridicule Nehemiah and his people faced did not discourage them. Nehemiah's path wasn't easy, but he was able to take the stones of hate, pain, and despair, pile them up, and rebuild the city—which gave his people hope.

I have spent many years collecting these stones, piling them up, and sulking over them in despair. I have been in various management positions in the corporate world over thirty years and came across many types of stones in the form of disrespect, racism, cultural alienation, and many others. The church is not immune from piles of stones in the way of growth. Sometimes, these stones are thrown at the leaders to discourage them from going forward. I took up several leadership positions in various churches and found out that there are even more severe stones. While being a boring speaker or incompetent at keeping track of projects are minor stones, there are major stones hurled at me of being irresponsible and even sometimes being plain rude. I was accused of not using the right judgment when making some decisions. I am sure everyone has this experience one time or other. Such stones may in the beginning bring bad feelings, but usually, at least one person once in a while would say,

"Thank you for being here." Those words of gratitude always outweighed whatever bad things others might have said. Those situations will bring the hurting stones back to life and hope.

Nehemiah was able to bring the stones back to life from the rubble-burned heaps. We read in chapter 4:4 that they "turned their insults back on their own heads." These stones hurt those who throw them more than they did others because they turn back on the throwers. We can ignore negativity and hatred. Joseph in the Old Testament is a great example of someone who turned stones into building blocks. He learned through the extreme difficulty he faced how to continue the journey. His brothers had rejected him and sold him to foreigners. Ultimately, his faith and integrity raised him to be the second in line to Pharaoh. His brothers had to go to him for help in time of famine. In Genesis 50:20, we read his final words to his brothers: "You meant evil, and God meant it for good."

As we face our stones, it is only by complete confidence in the goodness and plan of God that we can overcome them. What can destroy us can become building blocks on our journeys of faith as we look for the hand of God in all circumstances. "Our faith is the victory that overcomes the world" (1 John 5:4).

At times, we might find the stones of despair and exhaustion weighing us down and slowing our journeys. When times are difficult, the journey can seem never-ending.

But staying in it for the long run is extremely important. The people with Nehemiah were exhausted and frustrated. In Nehemiah 4:10, we read, "The strength of the laborers is giving out, and there is so much rubble that we cannot rebuild the wall." Nehemiah was a leader in that he encouraged them to stay in it for the long run.

A man walked into a lumberyard and said, "I need some four-by-twos."

The worker said, "You mean two-by-fours, don't you?"

"All right."

"How long do you need them?"

The man replied, "I need them for a long time."

We are in some life projects for a long time, and we will face stones of apathy, discouragement, despair, and exhaustion that are not easy to overcome, but we can learn to use those stones to build. When God is for us, who can be against us? Trust in a God who has given us the call: "We are more than conquerors through Christ who gives us strength."

Worries, doubt, and other cares of life can be stones that are more difficult to overcome than literal heaps of stones. In the book of Nehemiah chapter 5, we read about people complaining about their worries about food, taxes, debts, mortgages and on and on. In chapter 5 verse 5, we read, "We are powerless, because our fields and our vineyards belong to others." Giving God our best in the face of exhaustion is the key to success. David knew he was not going to be able to complete the temple, but he wanted to make sure that those who followed him would do a good job of finishing the temple. He said, "The house to be built for the Lord must be exceedingly magnificent" (1 Chronicles 22:5).

It is important that we do the best job we can with any opportunity we have. When I was part of a choir years ago, we had rehearsed a song for several weeks. There was one tricky section we just couldn't get right. We were ready to call it good enough. Being weary of rehearsing the same few measures over and over, someone said, "We've worked hard on this. We're tired, we're running short on time, and ninety-nine percent of the people won't know whether we sing it right." As we started to put away our music, the choir director said, "But we're going to sing it right for the one percent who know the difference." With a deep sigh we all reopened our music books. Giving our best in any effort will beat the stones of exhaustion and weariness.

Stones of condemnation and judgment are very common in Christian circles and groups. Some stones get thrown into a pile to be ignored or used later. Or are they unused ornaments? They are available to us just as they were to Nehemiah. We can be just as successful as he was if we make use of them. Nehemiah was not discouraged or frightened by circumstances or enemies. In chapter 4, we saw Sanballat, Tobiah, and Geshem mocking and ridiculing the workers, but as the work continued, they threatened them with physical violence. But the work continued, so in chapter 6, they tried to stop the work by using friendliness and persuasion.

A woman was brought to Jesus to be stoned and killed because she had been accused of adultery, the punishment for which was death. The religious leaders did not need recommendations from Jesus to do that. They were trying to trap Him. The stones they carried to throw at the woman were stones Jesus could use as well; He turned around and used the same stones against them by saying, "Those who have no sin may throw the first stone." Hearing this, they left one by one until the woman was alone with Jesus, who told her, "Neither do I condemn you." People carry stones around all the time, but some use them to build others up. Those who carried stones to throw at the woman were shamed by the One who was the cornerstone. If you carry a stone to throw, please leave it at the foot of Jesus today.

People were stoned for following their calling including Stephen, Paul, and other apostles. When we are discouraged, one of the things we can do is to reorganize our priorities and look at our lives. We should not be overcome or discouraged; we should do something about it! After looking everything over and sensing the discouragement in his team, Nehemiah rallied his troops in verse 14: "Don't be afraid of them. Remember the Lord, who is great and awesome." Nehemiah knew even in the face of opposition that the success of the wall was wholly dependent on God, who had inspired its beginning.

Verse 10 reminds the people that they could not rebuild the wall on their own. They needed to remember God and what He had promised. We read in chapter 4,

Then I said to the nobles, the officials and the rest of the people, "The work is extensive and spread out, and we are widely separated from each other along the wall. Wherever you hear the sound of the trumpet, join us there. Our God will fight for us!"

The apostle Paul reminded us in Ephesians 6:12, "Our struggle is not against flesh and blood, but against the spiritual forces of evil in the heavenly realms." They are the same spiritual forces of evil that are attacking Christians today. The strategies those spiritual forces used against God's people back then are still being used against Christians today.

Stones in our paths are inevitable, but we can choose how we will use them. We can build walls of difficulty or of success. We can use stones to build ourselves and others up. We can use our difficult, hurtful, sad stones as foundation stones for towers of misery or of joy that will give lasting hope to others.

God can use the stones in our lives to do greater things than we could ever do by ourselves. Our Father can use the stones in our lives to build wonderful foundations for us to stand on. He will tear down walls of stone that don't need to be up and reuse the stones to firm up existing foundations. Paul wrote in Philippians 1:6, "I am confident of this, that he who began a good work in you will carry it on to completion until the day of Christ Jesus."

# CHAPTER 13

# Arise and Cross

We had to go to a lawyer to discuss some legal matters. Before the meeting, my wife and I drafted some questions for him—what if this or that happens, what if there are liabilities, what if there is property damage, on and on. The lawyer read my notes, scribbled on them, and handed them back to me with a smile. He had answers to some, but for others, he wrote in big letters, "We will cross that bridge when we get there." There were more of those comments than answers.

That incident taught me some great lessons. One, he acknowledged that he didn't have answers to all our questions, but he knew that most of them would never need to be answered because many problems would likely not come up. If they did, we would handle them with what resources were available at that time. I think he was telling me nicely that he did not want to get paid for answering all my what-if questions but that he is getting paid for the what-now questions.

We want God to answer all our worry questions. But God says we should not worry about tomorrow because tomorrow will have its own worries. Today's troubles are enough for today. So let's just cross the bridge when we get there. What if there is no bridge? The book of Joshua shows the difficult task Joshua had; he and the people were at the brink of the flooding river, and they didn't have a bridge. What do you do when there is no bridge and the water is rising?

God had led them through the wilderness with a promise to take them to a good and spacious land flowing with milk and honey (Exodus 3:8). The Promised Land was in sight. The flooded Jordan stood between them and the Promised Land. The Bible tells us that they spent the next three days there. They all probably looked at the torrential flood with the roaring water with a sense of disappointment and desperation. Many of them lost faith and thought, *How can we cross this river with infants, with the sick, with the aged and all our animals, not to mention all our possessions strapped to wagons?* An insistent no began to form in their hearts as they listened to the roaring waters.

Many of us have heard the roar of floods in life. Sometimes, they can be so powerful that we don't even try to make it across. Our lives feel stalled, stuck on the wrong side. We wish we were on the other side. We read about the abundant life over there but cannot make it out of the wilderness. But if you look back, the experiences will testify that there is a God who is mightier than the roaring waters and flooding rivers. God can turn a no way into a highway. Our task is to arise and cross. Each of us has at least one story to share about small and big decisions we have had to make on our journeys. God has promised to be with us in all those decisions. I think of many who were challenged to venture into unknown territory. They waited patiently through all their ordeals—chemotherapy, radiation treatments, surgeries, and so on—and came through each with the faith and patience God equipped them with.

Churches can feel blocked from the promise of something great with God, but God is good all the time. At times, we may think we just cannot go on. Many saints before us have come to the flooding river, but they remained focused on the Promised Land and were determined to cross that river. Joshua 3 tells us something that is echoed throughout scripture: "What is impossible with men is possible with God" (Luke 18:27). God will reveal the steps we have to take in life so we can move from a stationary past to a dynamic future filled with adventures. God calls us to arise and cross.

More opportunities can mean more opposition. One decision is not the end of the journey. We have to cross the river; we have to face the walls of Jericho and the opposition of the people behind it. The Promised Land was home to Canaanites, Hittites, Amorites, Perizzites, Hivites, and Jebusites, who had homes, cities, and armies there. It would take more work and effort to win the battles to occupy the land.

The calling to a journey is an invitation to greater opportunities but stronger obstacles. Peter was asked to walk on water. Israelites were asked to wait so the water would dry out. What do you do when you're facing the impossible? Sometimes, you walk on water as Peter did, and other times, you walk through the water as Joshua and the people did.

One promise verse I like is Joshua 1:9: "Be strong and brave. Do not be terrified. Do not lose hope. I am the Lord your God. I will be with you everywhere you go." It has given me the strength to make important decisions about accepting jobs and moving to new places. God gives us opportunities, but we must step forward to claim them. God gives us the freedom to go any way we choose. He will show us the options, and we choose. It would be easy if God showed up in the middle of the night as he did to Mary and Joseph and told us exactly what to do, but that doesn't happen often.

In Luke 5, Jesus called four fishermen to go on an adventure, to pick up the cross and take the gospel to the ends of the world—to look out instead of in. The options in front of you may all be great opportunities, but you may not like any of them because you priorities are different. God is interested in your priorities as well. When you get married, when you buy a new home or accept a new job, what priorities guide you? Are they inward focused on self-gratification, wealth, and fame, or are they outward focused on becoming a blessing to others and bringing glory to God?

Many others have stood at the brink of flooding rivers in their journey that challenged what they believed in. William Carey, Hudson Taylor, John Wesley, and others came upon such flooding rivers in their journeys, but they decided to arise and cross them. We are also called to arise and cross in such situations. It can be at work or home, in dealing with relationships, or in our finances or health matters. Let us remember to give God thanks for helping us cross those rivers. All of us face such a moment or many such moments in our lives that challenge us to shift our focus to something greater and larger than us.

There is a river we all will cross alone one day before we enter eternity. There is no choice on that journey. All living beings will have to cross over the valley of death, a cold river roaring with fierceness that can intimidate us if we don't have faith. Thank God Jesus has already crossed death ahead of us. By the grace of God, we can cross that raging river, and God promises to be with us in the valley of the shadow of death. Because of Jesus, the waters have no choice but to subside. He has given rest to those who believe in Him, and He will carry them on His shoulders to the place He has prepared for them.

Our corruptible selves will become incorruptible; our

mortal selves will become immortal. "Death is swallowed up in victory. O Death, where is your sting? O Hell, where is your victory? Thanks be to God, who gives us the victory through our Lord Jesus Christ" (1 Corinthians 15:54–57).

Samuel Stennett (1727–1795) wrote the blessed hymn "On Jordan's Stormy Banks I Stand." He wrote that our true possession lies in Canaan—heaven—and not on the earthly side of the Jordan. He was determined to cross it: "I cast a wishful eye, I am bound for the Promised Land." Canaan is a land of wide, extended plains where eternal day is always shining, where God the Son reigns. "No chilling winds or poisonous breath can reach that healthful shore" where there is no more "sickness and sorrow, pain and death" and I cannot wait to get there and "see the Father's face."

I remember an old Sunday school song: "Heaven is a wonderful place, filled with glory and grace, I want to see my savior's face." Heaven is the wonderful place where the journeys end.

Printed in the United States
By Bookmasters